EDMUND SPENSER

EDMUND SPENSER

An Essay
on Renaissance Poetry

BY

W. L. RENWICK, M.A., D.Litt.

REGIUS PROFESSOR OF RHETORIC
AND ENGLISH LITERATURE
IN THE UNIVERSITY OF EDINBURGH

LONDON
EDWARD ARNOLD (PUBLISHERS) LTD.

Printed in Great Britain by
Lowe & Brydone (Printers) Limited, London, N.W.10

TO
MY WIFE

Contents

EDMUND SPENSER

Introduction

In the following chapters an attempt is made to arrive at some understanding of what a very important poet was trying to do and why he was trying to do that and not something else, of the reasons why his poems have their peculiar form and character. Some such understanding is necessary to any critic, whether his aim be judgment, as with Johnson, or philosophy, as with Arnold ; nor is it useless even to those who, like Hazlitt, look upon criticism as the expression of a personal mood.

This implies historical study, and also the careful direction of that study. All the facts of an artist's life and surroundings are useful to the student who wishes to understand his work, for the circumstances and conditions within which that work was done naturally affect and modify even where they do not completely control it. We never can know all the facts : there always must be circumstances round the birth of any work of art unknown to anyone but the artist himself, and perhaps even ignored by him—small material and physical accidents as well as moral and spiritual and emotional accidents, temporary, and insufficient to affect the general substance of his art, but for the time of their action efficient causes in the production and modification of the work in progress. Nor are all the facts, even if we knew

1

them all, of equal importance.   There are circumstances which, prominent though they may be in the life of the day, have very little effect upon the artist's life of thought, upon his methods of work, or upon the quality of his art ; the knowledge of other circumstances may help the student to understand the subject or sympathize with the mood of a particular work ; for the critic the really important facts are those which prescribed the general scheme of the artist's work as a whole, and prescribed his attitude to his art, to his age, and to the world.

Thus the promotion of Spenser from Clerk of Degrees and Recognisances to the Irish Court of Chancery to Clerk of the Council of Munster may have meant that he had more or less time to spend on *The Faerie Queene*, but made no difference to the subject, the plan, or the style of the great poem.   The chain of accidents which led to his meeting with Raleigh culminated in *Colin Clouts Come Home Again*, but did not make that poem a pastoral.   To know the true name of the lady Rosalind with whom he was in love is not really valuable to the student, unless the discoverer of that elusive lady should also discover some peculiarity of temper in her which left a permanent influence on the poet's work—not only on subject, for the verb *amo, I love*, is the same to whomsoever it be conjugated, but on treatment and tone. Gossip is always interesting and often helpful, but only in secondary matters, and in no study is it less helpful than in that of the greater poets of the Renaissance.

In treating historical and biographical facts the student must consider both the artist he studies and the kind of study he professes.   The journeys of Chaucer, for instance, of Smollett, and of Byron, are documents of different kinds.   The profession of biography is concerned with the man, that of commentary with the details of particular works, that of criticism with the greater facts which made or modified the whole of the artist's creation. The life of Spenser has been written, so far as it is known—that is, in its main events—and the poems have been related to the life ; it would be futile to add another and necessarily weaker performance of a task so gracefully accomplished of late by M. Emile Legouis. If greater detail is desired than the facts of birth, marriage, employment, and so forth, there is matter enough to be elucidated, and American scholars especially have done admirable service in attempting to solve the series of problems presented by the personal and political allusions so thickly strewn throughout all Spenser's poems.[1] No further solutions need be expected here. In the first place, many of these allusions are extremely obscure. Their interpretation is uncertain and liable to be upset by chance discovery, and so any deductions except the most obvious are insecure and possibly dangerous. That may not absolve the biographer from the attempt, but as their very obscurity proves, these allusions were intended for Spenser's contemporaries, not for posterity, and are therefore of secondary moment for the critic of his art. It is more necessary for us to understand why they are there than to puzzle out what they mean. Nor is it likely that they will shed light on more than fragments of Spenser's work and thought.

The critic's business is to select from the available

[1] If few or no references are given to earlier workers in the field, it is because their labours are so exhaustively catalogued by Dr. Frederick Ives Carpenter in his invaluable *Outline Guide to Edmund Spenser*, and because the writer would not be thought to shelter behind authority.

body of documents those greater facts which mould and colour all the artist's work. Now, we cannot draw near to Spenser through knowledge of external events, as we can to Wordsworth, or through biography, as we can to Byron and Cowper. Yet the artist must build his work round something : he does not function in a vacuum. His incentive—or opportunity—may be given by political institutions, as to Cicero or Velasquez ; by social conditions, as to Dowland or Addison or Reynolds ; by religious forms, as to Giotto or Palestrina or Sophocles or Bossuet. All these things, of course, affect every artist, but in the formation of Spenser's art the central fact, after his time and nationality and as the corollary to these, is his scholarly training. A catalogue of his library would tell us far more than a list of his official positions about the most 'literary' poet, except his follower Milton, in the English language. We must regard his work as part of a cultural movement of European extent, as fruit of general and not merely personal experience. For Spenser himself so regarded it. Beyond all personal interests he was facing the problem of how good English poetry might be written—English poetry that might vie with the Greek and Latin and Italian and French poetry which men proclaimed with one accord to be good poetry. It is more than a question of 'influences' and 'sources.' We do not speak of the 'influence' of the elder Burbage on Shakespeare, though the man who built the Theatre prescribed the form of *Hamlet* : so also the theories and precedents, and the doctrine of respect for them, are the primary facts in the study of Spenser's poetry.

It might be argued that the significance of Spenser's personal history lies in its negations, for it was his fortune to be refused the peaceful life in England that he desired. He was at the birth of Elizabethan poetry, but his duties in Ireland kept him out of the centre for the rest of his life. He was a scholar-poet on a disturbed frontier, an Englishman in Ireland, an official, subject to official restraints in thought and action. He retained his scholarly interests—he could not cease to be a poet—grew to like the country, as has happened to exiled Englishmen since, seems to have been a useful and capable official—more efficient than his poetic master Ariosto showed himself in his brief tenure of office in the Garfagnana. But if he had been as fortunate at court as Ronsard, if he had never gone to Ireland, though he might have celebrated some other hill than Arlo, seen his swarm of gnats over the Cambridge fens instead of the Bog of Allen, married another lady than Elizabeth Boyle, he would probably have continued the Heroic Poem he began before 1580, and continued it on much the same lines. A poet is not a passive body impinged on by external forces, and Spenser was a man of positive mind who chose his own way. The mark of an ' influence ' is the record of an affinity ; the exploitation of a ' source ' is an indication of taste or reason, or both. Also the humanist training stayed with a man : witness Milton, returning after twenty stormy years to fulfil the ambitions it had planted in him, a changed man, perhaps, but with his literary ideals unaltered.

This present study, accordingly, is concerned with ideas more than with events—or rather with a certain body of ideas whose assimilation was the most important event in the artistic life of this particular poet—and most of all with those ideas about the way of writing which Spenser would learn from his masters and discuss with

his friends at school and University. Critical theories
are dealt with in greater detail than philosophical or political, not only because they are less accessible to the average student, but because that body of critical thought
which formed Spenser's poetry, after being the common
basis of literary teaching for two centuries, has been
forgotten, or at least obscured, in a hundred years of
'romantic' criticism. The details may seem dull and
stupid, just as our arguments will a hundred years hence,
but they were interesting to Spenser and his time, and
they helped to make Elizabethan poetry. They may
be the more despised at this present moment because
they are largely technical ; they were then the more
useful to that most studious of literary craftsmen. Spenser had to study the craft of letters, for his time required
it, and much of his work might be called, without dis-
paragement, literary exercise. That is one of many
reasons why he is what Charles Lamb called him, the
Poets' Poet. Like every good artist he is at times preoccupied with technique, and, as with every good artist,
any piece of work is at one and the same time a record
of thought and feeling and a technical exercise. The
most fatal error of the criticism of last century was its
tendency to regard the study of technique as uninterest-
ing, unimportant, even intrusive, whereas it can be so
only if it is made so.

No thesis is advanced in these pages, for a thesis often
excludes more than it includes, and may be pursued for
ends not truly literary. The end and aim of all our
study is in the poems of Spenser, not in the detail
of biography or in the minutiæ of Tudor politics, still
less in science or metaphysics. It is not contended
even that the critics quoted, and none but they, formed

the mind of Spenser—otherwise the omission of reference to Scaliger, for instance, would be strange history—they are those the writer considers most appropriate (in an essay whose brevity demands a certain economy in argument) to represent a whole school of critical thought, just as the name of Chaucer represented the whole tradition and covered many things not his in the early editions. In any case we do not know with certainty what Spenser read and what he did not, especially as he had excellent opportunities in his youth for making acquaintance with ancient and modern literature both native and foreign, and the most important critical 'sources' of all cannot be recovered—the oral teaching in school and University, the discussions with Harvey in Cambridge rooms and walks, with Sidney and Dyer and Greville at such meetings as Bruno described in his *Cena de le Cenere*, and with later friends even in Ireland, as Ludovic Bryskett tells in his *Discourse of Civill Life*. Nor is any attempt made at a final judgment of Spenser and his work. The better understanding, and through understanding the better appreciation of his poetic ideas, aims, and methods is the humbler business of this book.

The reader is conjured to remember what the writer has felt throughout his study, though for lack of knowledge, imagination, and skill he fail to convey it—the heat of enthusiasm in which the new poetry of the sixteenth century was wrought, the eagerness with which materials and methods of treatment were sought and discussed, and the energy and devotion of the men who gave England her share of poetic glory: and if any comparisons with problems and tasks of modern poetry arise in his mind, so much the better.

CHAPTER I

The New Poetry of the Sixteenth Century

The fifteenth-century revival of the classics must have originated in some dissatisfaction with existing literature and current scholarship. Only half conscious, it may be, of what was wrong, men felt that even their greatest—Dante, Guillaume de Lorris, Aquinas, Occam —lacked something they needed, something which, by a fortunate instinct, they sought and found in Virgil, in Cicero, in Plato. Then, having found a literature which satisfied their instincts, they set to work to make more of it for themselves. The fifteenth century is the century of the latinists, the imitators. The best prose, they argued, was that of Cicero, the best verse that of Virgil ; the obvious way, then, to write well was to follow them, and the more closely one's work resembled theirs, the better one was writing. This meant reproduction rather than creation, and could not satisfy for ever, the more that, in their eager admiration and no less eager endeavour to be worthy followers of the best, the humanists not only denied virtue to anything that was not Greek or Latin, but, by setting up Cicero and Virgil and Catullus as the authentic examples of the only way Latin might be written, they killed Latin as a literary medium, since without the right to an individual style no author could completely express his individuality.

As the century drew on, the charm of novelty and the

9

excitement of discovery faded. Linguistic, grammatical, and formal criticism, though still an active interest, became commonplaces of the schools, and the virtue of humanist imitation began to wear thin. Truer appreciation, perhaps, revealed that the fashionable imitation reproduced only external accidents, while the true object of delight and source of satisfaction escaped its grasp, and common sense at last revealed to ambition that it was impossible to compete with men who had their Greek or their Latin familiarly, as their mother tongue. Indeed the humanists were not really competing, except with one another for the prize of the most complete servility —and all the while the painters and sculptors and architects, who had recovered enough of classical art to teach and inspire, but not so much, as yet, as to hamper them, were showing that the modern world also had its triumphs and its magnificences. The world felt full of power, and with a just pride in the activity of the new age, began to resent the arrogance of men who, comparatively sterile themselves, based their exclusive claim to consideration upon their knowledge of the activity of a dead past.

Petrarch, the leader of the eager band of humanists, is also, it is true, one of the great modern poets of Italy, but the success of his Tuscan poetry, and the revival of its influence more than a century after his death, have somewhat obscured the fact that it belongs to a pre-Renaissance tradition. His *Rime* lead back to the twelfth century as well as forward to the sixteenth. He himself regarded them as minor offspring of his genius ; his real work, the work for which the men of his own time crowned him with laurel in the Capitol, was in Latin—the *Africa*, the Eclogues, the Dialogues and Epistles, imitations of

Virgil and Cicero. In the later fifteenth century Politian and Lorenzo de' Medici treated of classical themes in Tuscan, but their poems, with all their grace and sweetness, are but the best of social and festival verses, relaxations from severer studies or condescensions on popular or courtly gaiety. But at the end of the century, when Cardinal Bembo recommended him to follow up his early successes in Latin poetry, Ludovico Ariosto replied that he would rather be one of the first among Tuscan poets than even the second among latinists. Here was a deliberate choice between Latin and the vernacular, and the decision meant the arrival of a new poetry, made in the modern tongues by men trained in the classical school, a poetry which, once Ariosto had shown its power, grew to challenge not only the imitations of the classics, but the classics themselves.

By the time the humanist impulse reached France and England, the imitation of classical prose and verse had been carried to a high perfection by generations of Italian scholars. Success was not so easy in the face of the standard set, nor was the mere possession of the classical tongues a sufficient source of pride now that they were more common. Besides, the freshness of the adventure had worn off. To a scholar of the time of Petrarch it was a high endeavour to attempt the re-creation of the Virgilian epic and the Ciceronian dialogue ; he could feel the inspiration of belonging to the mighty company of the ancients. By the sixteenth century the thing had been done about as well as might be. New efforts would naturally be measured against Bembo and Sadoleto and Pontanus rather than against Cicero and Virgil, and these, however respectable and even venerable, were not such exciting colleagues for youth ambitious of the laurel. The strong and original mind desired wider fields for achievement than what was after all but a scholarly accomplishment, and desired a greater prize—fame and immortality, not the professional esteem of the pedagogues. Latin might be upheld as the only language for the learned, but not as the only language for the poet. Latin poetry was cultivated, and successfully, but it could not be a real danger to vernacular poetry, for the position was already given away in Italy, the native country of humanism, and the new Tuscan poetry—the second wave of humanism—closely followed on the first in the movement north.

In any case the new scholarly interest in the vernacular met and blended with a new political interest north of Avignon, and received thereby an inestimable reinforcement, since the greatest source of power in a language is its political implication. Dante had advocated the establishment of an ' illustrious, cardinal, courtly, and curial ' Italian as part of a campaign for the re-establishment of a Roman empire, defeated by the separatist tendencies of the Communes. The tradition of the might of Rome which still lingered round its visible remains was a powerful factor in the first revival of the classics, just as, conversely, Petrarch's sympathy for the abortive republic of Rienzi grew from the literary tradition of the ancient civic virtues in his beloved Cicero. But the sixteenth-century interest in the vernacular was purely a literary interest. Trissino's translation of Dante's treatise *de Vulgari Eloquio*, published in 1529, may have helped to make the position which Ariosto had already taken up respectable, but the political argument of Dante's first Book was useless to a divided Italy broken by foreign invasions, and the critics upheld the Tuscan dialect against his authority, on the ground of the literary excellence it had achieved.

Outside Italy the sentiment of Rome might be felt in the mind, its tragedy in the heart, but it was not in the blood. The respect due to ancestry was given to the broken-down mediæval system, and from the ruins of that system there was rising a social and political force which in Italy was only a dream of the elder poets —the new spirit of nationalism. The fading of Petrarch's dream of a Rome reborn among her ashes was perhaps a contributory cause of the new interest taken by his followers of a hundred years later in the Italian vernacular—and indeed literature has always been the first trench and the last ditch of Italian politics—certainly in France and England the sense of nationality, strong and growing even among humanists who professed an international culture, found its natural symbol in the national speech. ' Doubt not,' wrote Ronsard in 1565, ' but if there were still in France Dukes of Burgundy, of Picardy, of Normandy, of Brittany, of Champagne, of Gascony, they would desire, for the honour of their grandeur, that their subjects should write in the tongue of their native country. For Princes should not be less careful to extend their language among all nations than to enlarge the bounds of their empire.' [1] Fifteen years later, Gabriel Harvey echoes Ronsard in a letter to Spenser, in which he is obviously stating ironically some of Spenser's own views : ' What thoughe it hath bene the practisse of the floorishingest States and most politique commonwelthes . . . to make the very most of ther vulgar tunges, and togither with there seignioryes and dominions by all meanes possible to amplifye and enlarge them, devisinge

[1] *Abrégé de l'Art Poétique François*, ed. Blanchemain, VIII, p. 320.

all ordinarye and extraordinarye helpes, both for the polisshinge and refining of them at home, and alsoe for the spreddinge and dispersinge of them abroade ? ' [1]

The true line of defence was discovered by Sperone Speroni in his *Dialogo delle Lingue*, published in 1543. In that treatise one of the speakers reports an argument between Peretto, a teacher in Bologna, and the humanist Lascaris, who cannot believe that philosophy is possible in a modern tongue. Peretto is represented as arguing thus : ' I hold firmly, that the tongues of every country, Arabian and Indian as Roman and Athenian, are of equal value, and formed by mortal men for a purpose, through judgment. You should not speak of them as a thing produced by nature, for they are made and regulated by the artifice of the peoples after their own will, not planted or sown. . . . Languages are not born like trees or herbs, this weak and infirm of kind, that solid and robust and fit to bear the weight of our human conceptions, but all their qualities are born into the world at the will of mortals. . . . No tongue in the world, be it what you will, can have of itself the power to signify the conceptions of our minds, but all lies in the will of the peoples.' [2] This is the charter of the vernaculars. In the first manifesto of the new poetry in France, *La Deffence et Illustration de la Langue Françoyse*, Joachim du Bellay, quoting (without acknowledgment) even the phrases of Speroni,[3] makes this doctrine one of the bases of his plea for the cultivation of French. The other base is the sentiment of nationality : the speech of so great a people and coun-

---

[1] *Elizabethan Critical Essays*, ed. Gregory Smith, I, 123.

[2] Edition of 1596, p. 123.

[3] Livre I, chap. i. See Pierre Villey, *Une Source Italienne de la Deffence et Illustration.*

try may not be called barbarous, and if it be deficient, it ought to be studied and improved by those whose mother tongue it is. The point was pressed home with characteristic vigour by his colleague Ronsard.

In England, these same arguments reappear in a place of peculiar significance, in the writings of Richard Mulcaster, a strong and original character who was principal master of the Merchant Taylors School when Spenser was a scholar there. *The First Part of the Elementarie* was published in 1582, thirteen years after Spenser had gone to Cambridge, but Mulcaster, like every schoolmaster, was writing from long experience, and we may presume that Spenser was taught on somewhat these lines. Mulcaster lays it down that the schoolboy should be trained in the reading, writing,[1] and grammar of the mother tongue, which is not to be despised as rude and incapable. ' The finest tung, was once in filth, the verie course of natur proceding from weaknesse, to strength from imperfection to perfitnesse, from a mean degree, to a main dignitie.' [2] ' No one tung is more fine then other naturallie, but by industrie of the speaker, which . . . endevoreth himself to garnish it with eloquence, and to enrich it with learning. . . . And therefor the learned tungs so termd of their store, maie thank their own people, both for their fining at home, and their favor abrode. Whereupon it falleth out, that as we ar profited by the mean of these tungs, so we are to honor them even for profit sake, and yet not so but that we maie cherish our own, both in such cases, as the use

---

[1] Care is required in quoting Mulcaster : when he speaks of ' the right writing of our English tung ' he means ' the proper spelling.' Orthography was a problem of the time in every country in Europe.
[2] P. 62.

thereof is best : and in such places, as it maie be bettered, tho with imparing of them.   For did not those tungs use even the same means to brave themselves ear theie proved so beawtifull ?   Did the peple strain curtesie to pen in their naturall, even these same arguments which theie had from the foren ?   If theie had don so, we had never had their works, whereat we wonder so.'[1]

'For the account of our tung, both in pen and speche, no man will dout thereof, who is able to judge what those things be, which make anie tung to be of account, which things I take to be three, the authoritie of the peple which speak it, the matter and argument, wherein the speche dealeth, the manifold use, for which the speche serveth.   For all which three, our tung nedeth not to give place, to anie of her peres.   First to saie somewhat for the peple, that use the tung, the English nation hath allwaie bene of good credit, and great estimation, ever since credit and estimation by historie came on this side the Alps. . . .   Next for the argument, wherein it dealeth, whether privat or publik, it maie compare with som other, that think verie well of their own selves. . . . Will matters of war, whether civill or foren, make a tung of account ?   Our neighbour nations will not deny our peple to be very warrious, and our own cuntrie will confesse it. . . .   Will all kindes of trade, and all sorts of traffik, make a tung of account ?   If the spreading sea, and the spacious land could use anie speche, theie would both show you, where, and in how manie strange places, theie have sene our peple, and also give you to wit, that theie deal in as much, and as great varietie of matters, as anie other peple do, whether at home or abrode.   Which is the reason why our tung doth serve

[1] P. 253.

to so manie uses, bycause it is conversant with so manie
peple, and so well acquainted with so manie matters, in
so manie sundrie kindes of dealing.'[1]

' Our *English* wits be verie well able, thanks be to God,
if their wils were as good, to make those uncouth and
unknown learnings verie familiar to our peple, even in
our own tung.'[2]   ' The diligent labor of learned cuntriemen did so enrich these tungs and not the tungs them
selves, tho theie proved verie pliable, as our tung will
prove, I dare assure it of knowledge, if our learned
cuntriemen will put to their labor.'[3]

Ascham had apologized manfully enough for writing
Toxophilus in English :   ' And althoughe to have written
this boke either in latin or Greke (which thing I wold be
verie glad yet to do, if I might surelie know your Graces
pleasure there in) had been more easier and fit for mi
trade in study, yet neverthelesse, I supposinge it no point
of honestie, that mi commodity should stop and hinder
ani parte either of the pleasure or profite of manie, have
written this Englishe matter in the Englishe toungue
for Englishe men.'[4]   Mulcaster's honest common sense
will have none of this scholarly coquetting with the business : ' I do write in my naturall English toungue, bycause
though I make the learned my judges, which understand
Latin, yet I meane good to the unlearned, which understand but English. . . .   He that understands no Latin
can understand English, and he that understands Latin
very well, can understand English farre better, if he will
confesse the trueth, though he thinke he have the habite

---

[1] P. 80.   Cf. du Bellay, *Deff. et Ill.*, ed. Person, p. 156.
[2] P. 255.
[3] P. 255.
[4] Dedication to Henry VIII : ed. Arber, p. 14.   Cf. p. 18.

and can Latin it exceeding well.'[1] ' For is it not in dede
a marvellous bondage, to becom servants to one tung for
learning sake, the most of our time, with losse of most
time, whereas we maie have the verie same treasur in our
own tung, with the gain of most time ? our own bearing
the joyfull title of our libertie and fredom, the *Latin*
tung remembering us, of our thraldom and bondage ?
I love *Rome*, but *London* better, I favor *Italie*, but *England*
more, I honor the *Latin*, but I worship the *English*.'[2]

These are scholars' arguments for the ' disciplines,'
the science and philosophy whose value lies in their
import and which may be had in all dialects. Poetry,
however, is an art ; the new poetry had to acquire a
manner, and could not leave form and style a monopoly
of its latinist competitors. In the main portion of
Speroni's Dialogue, which is concerned with the language of poetry, Cardinal Bembo is presented as one
of the interlocutors, and Speroni puts into his mouth
a resumé of his own writings on the subject. Bembo
was a notable latinist, renowned as a scrupulous Ciceronian, and when he was converted to the cause of the
vernaculars—a valuable accession of strength and prestige—he changed masters, but not methods. Trained
in the imitation of Cicero and Virgil, he substituted for
these names the names of Boccaccio and Petrarch, and
continued on the old lines. ' When it happens,' he
wrote in his essay *della Volgar Lingua*, ' that the manner

---

[1] *Positions*, 1581 ; ed. Quick, pp. 2–3. Mulcaster was evidently a
notorious heretic, if we may judge from the entry of this book in the
Stationers' Register with the proviso ' that yf this booke conteine any
thinge prejudiciall or hurtfull to the book of maister Askham that was
printed by master Daie called the Scholemayster, that then this lycense shal
be voyd.'

[2] *Elementarie*, p. 254.

of speech of past times is better than that of the present, then we ought to write in the style of past times and not in that of our own. For if Seneca and Tranquilla and Lucan and Claudian, and all those writers that have been since the time of Julius Cæsar and Augustus, and since that fair and happy age down to our own day, had written in the manner of their elders, of Virgil I mean and Cicero, they would have written much better and more praise-worthy prose and verse than they would have written in their own manner ; and we also will do much better if we discourse in our papers in the style of Boccaccio and Petrarch than we shall do by discoursing in our own style.'[1] Speroni gave Bembo the last word in his argument about the Italian dialects, refuting the Courtier who advocated the common Italian of Dante's *de Vulgari Eloquio* : ' Allowing that Peretto's opinion is true, that the countryman can talk philosophy as well as the gentle-man, the Roman as well as the Lombard, it is not the case that poetry or oratory can be written in every language equally, since one among them may be better endowed with the ornaments of prose and verse than another. . . . I tell you again, that if the desire ever comes upon you to compose either *canzoni* or *novelle* in your own way, that is in a dialect other than Tuscan and without imi-tating Petrarch or Boccaccio, perhaps you may make a good courtier, but a poet, or an orator, never.'

Thus the ' Bembists ' made or discovered no new principle ; they retraversed the fifteenth century to take up that Tuscan part of Petrarch's legacy, which had been neglected by all but very minor poets, and they were fortunate in finding a poet and a prose-writer of indubitable greatness, impressive by reason of a hundred

[1] *Prose,* ed. of 1547, fol. 23.

years' reputation, yet belonging to the modern world and leaders of the modern scholarship. The renown of Petrarch and Boccaccio as humanists could be held to protect their vernacular works from the most prejudiced latinist. The language had changed so little that it was possible to take their works as a standard and to apply to others the humanistic tests of ' purity ' and ' correctness ' in relation to them. Above all, there was nothing in the spirit or tone or ideals of their work which definitely marked them as belonging to a different age, or which conflicted with the spirit or the ideals of a hundred years later.

The movement back to the classics began in Italy. Dissatisfaction with what the Middle Ages had accomplished was bound to begin there, for the social and political system which we think of as the characteristic creation of the Middle Ages was the creation of France and England, and hardly touched Italy, so that there the literature which expressed the ideals of that system was always an alien thing. Dante is indeed the greatest of mediaeval poets, but represents only the academic side of the Middle Ages, their philosophy and theology. It is his distinction that he made great Italian poetry out of matters which otherwise appear only in Latin treatises ; the subjects and methods of mediaeval French poetry neither attract nor influence him, for though he and his friends learned so much from the school of Provençal love-poets, they transformed what they took by developing it in a purely intellectual medium, quite apart from the social institutions within which it was invented. Dante's politics are party politics, not the personal and dynastic quarrellings of the feudal lands ; his political thought centres round the idea of the Empire, the one portion of mediaeval theory which was least operative in France and England. The whole history of the Italian towns as from communes they became duchies, and the whole development of society within them from the intercourse of burgess families to the state of courts, run counter to the history of the North. True mediaeval romance died a natural death with the feudal society whose ideals and interests it expressed, but while Malory was writing the last romance in England, Boiardo was writing the first in Italy, and he and Ariosto gave it a new lease of life amid new conditions, just as Petrarch did to Provençal love-song. While in the north Romance was being degraded in chapbooks and street ballads, they rescued it from the ballad-mongers, through whom it was becoming popular in Italy, and raised it to a new status. To Ariosto it was a new form, neither constrained by its old social function nor contaminated by the memory of old conflicts ; to the North it was an old-fashioned and well-worn thing, to him fresh and full of opportunities for an enterprising artist. He took the form as he found it, made an artistic version of the interrupted recitation of the professional storyteller of the market-place, ballasted it with somewhat of learned discipline, enriched it with his own ebullient spirit and the magnificence of courtly Ferrara, and sent it North again to inspire a new generation.

Humanism occupied Italy without conflict, for there was practically nothing there to conflict with it. When the new poetry arrived with Ariosto it had only classicist criticism to face. But in the north they both met the body of mediaeval habits and traditions and prejudices which remained powerful though the system in which they had evolved was all but destroyed. A Pope like

Nicholas V patronized humanism ; the Faculty of Theology entrenched in the Sorbonne opposed it violently. Humanism conquered, and in time brought forth the new poetry of ' la Pléiade ' ; but that new poetry had in its turn to make its way against the relics of the mediaeval—a school of poetry with its own canons and its own ideals, and with a formidable mass of accomplishment behind it. To this the more narrow-minded nationalists clung. It meant the past of France, it was the achievement of France ; and though the wiser minds hailed the new thought with joy, they could not bury the past without regret—yet burial was necessary. In his Ode to Jaques Pelletier Ronsard remembers :

> La Rose si bien escrite,
> Et contre les femmes despite,
> Par qui je fus en enfance enchanté,

but its faded imagery appears hardly at all in his work. His friend Binet tells how in his youth Ronsard ' had ever in hand some French poet whom he read with judgment, and principally (as he himself has often told me) a Jean Lemaire de Belges, a Romance of the Rose, and the works of Clément Marot.' But though du Bellay and Ronsard loved the old poets of their country, and though they had been brought up to regard imitation as normal, they could not put these men in the place in which Bembo had put Petrarch and Boccaccio. They saw clearly enough that the learning, thought, and style of the Rose were alike superseded, that Jean Lemaire was not artist enough to serve any longer as a model, that Marot, undisciplined in construction and entangled in the wilful difficulties of worn-out verse-forms, was neither scholar enough nor serious enough for modern

needs. ' Whoso wishes to enrich his language, let him
set himself to the imitation of the best Greek and Latin
authors : and direct the point of his style to all their
greatest virtues, as to a sure goal.' [1] ' Since the amplifi-
cation of our language cannot be accomplished without
learning and without erudition, I would warn those who
aspire to that glory to imitate the good Greek and Latin
authors, not to speak of Italian, Spanish, and others.' [2]

The young Ronsard had Virgil also ' ever in hand ' ;
and Virgil was really more modern than Jean de Meung.
The discovery of the classics was the discovery of a
literature which satisfied certain desires, vague and obscure
but intense and serious, which the mediaeval tradition
could no longer satisfy. The poets of the Pléiade set
themselves to give such literature to France. It was
an additional spur to their patriotism that Italy was
already in the field. They had to seek their models
abroad, and with simple strategy they made their necessity a virtue and announced it as a principle that imitation ' within the language ' was valueless. [3] The
counter-currents of keen scholarship, national pride, and
modernist self-assertion met and balanced in a group of
men who were by nature—let us not forget it—great
artists, and out of the clash came the new poetry of
France.

The virtue of the delightfully and infectiously enthu-
siastic criticism of the Pléiade lies in its balance and its
width of outlook—less in its transference of classical
matter and ideals into the vernacular than in its firm hold
on the vernacular amid all the excitement of the discovery

[1] *Deff. et Ill.*, p. 71.
[2] *Deff. et Ill.*, p. 109.
[3] *Deff. et Ill.*, p. 72.

of greater worlds. The new poets were classicists, but they were Frenchmen, and men of their century. They saw that while tradition may be a living force it may, be it classicist or mediaeval, become a dead weight, and they reacted, not from the past, but from those contemporaries who could not see or would not acknowledge that it was the past—the past of Virgil or the past of Jean de Meung. The essential thing was neither a language nor a tradition, but the making of poetry. Nor was it merely that they cultivated the vernacular : they set out to do in and for their native speech what the ancients had done in theirs, and, always with reverence for the ancients, they claimed for their work equal consideration.

It was not that Ariosto in Italy and Ronsard in France were the first to infuse something of the classics into vernacular literature. But Ariosto was the first of the humanists' pupils to take Tuscan as seriously as Latin. Ronsard followed a generation involved in vapid mediaevalism, to whom the new learning only provided new vices to add to their already considerable stock. England profited by their experience. Humanism had come with Colet and Linacre and More, the Bembist revival of Petrarchan fashion with Wyatt and Surrey. By Spenser's time, the latinists were no longer very serious rivals and, on the other hand, classical learning, manipulated and familiarized by a whole dynasty of Cambridge humanists, could be assimilated as it could not be by Skelton, in whom a new culture and a dying (but not dead) tradition were ever at war. Spenser knew what had been done in Italy, and was fired to emulation and encouraged in his ambition. He had before his eyes the example of France, newly made illustrious by men yet living, by a group of poets whose situation and whose problems were almost exactly his own, and whose experience, solutions, and methods were clearly set forth by themselves. He was the pupil of a man who belonged to the same school of thought as the Pléiade and shared many of their ideas, and while under his care he translated certain sonnets of du Bellay for Jean van der Noodt, a fanatical propagandist of Ronsard and the new poetry. Long afterwards, when he was a poet of established position, he was still sufficiently interested to remodel these translations and add a eulogy of his original. The admirer of du Bellay could not fail to know of Ronsard, so often hailed by du Bellay, in verse and prose, as friend and chieftain, and however political and religious antagonism made odious the apologist of the Massacre of St. Bartholomew and fierce defender of Mary Queen of Scots, Philip Sidney must have talked of the great French poet who was in high favour at the court of Charles IX during his sojourn in Paris. Gascoigne's *Certayne Notes of Instruction*, the only critical treatise (as distinct from textbooks of formal rhetoric) published in England before *The Shepheardes Calender*, is in large part a version—lacking, it is true, some of the most characteristic and challenging passages—of Ronsard's *Abrégé de l'Art Poétique François*, and every English critic down to Ben Jonson shows evident signs of acquaintance with the French ideas. Spenser could not fail to know this movement, and could not fail to be interested.

Spenser did not suffer like the Pléiade from the patriotic upholder of the mediaeval. Chaucer, indeed, who embodied that tradition for sixteenth-century England, was not only easily available in printed editions, but was popular and even fashionable. Chaucer was the one Englishman who could be acclaimed a master poet.

He was too great to be ignored by any young Englishman who aspired to poetic rank, and Spenser imitated him as Ronsard imitated no French predecessor. Yet he was too far off to be any danger to the new age. He belonged to a dead past, his language obsolete in syntax as well as in vocabulary, the secret of his verse lost. The spirit and doctrine of his poetry, though still intelligible and admirable, were definitely and unmistakably those of a different social, political and cultural epoch, in part no longer applicable to life, and lacking many interests of importance to the England of Elizabeth. Above all, the Reformation had set a barrier between the fourteenth-century poet and the poet of the sixteenth. No one could demand that the younger man should follow the elder any more closely than Spenser did : indeed the claims of the new age were so strong as to make his affectation of Chaucerism rather a matter of reproach, in certain circles, than of praise.

The poetry of the late sixteenth century could not be a mere continuation of the poetry of the Middle Ages, now superseded by the greater poetry of antiquity ; yet since that greater poetry was now firmly established, the charm of the mediaeval could be appreciated, and even cultivated, without dangerous implications. Ascham had denounced Chaucer along with Malory, romance, and the Middle Ages generally, but the younger generation rather adopted him. Their reasons were not the opposite of Ascham's reasons for denunciation, but new reasons of their own. Thus the scholar Gabriel Harvey, Spenser's friend, noted in the margin of his copy of *Dionysius Periegetes* : ' Chaucer and Lidgate ; fine artists in many kinds, and much better learned than owre modern poets.' ' Other commend Chaucer and

Lidgate for their witt, pleasant veine, and all humanitie :
I specially their astronomie, philosophie, and other parts
of profound or cunning art.   Wherein few of their time
were more exactly learned.'[1]

The praise of the old poets as scholars and philosophers
is the measure of the new and more serious interest in
poetry which was one of the fruits of humanism.   The
new poets regarded their own work, not as secondary or
subaltern, but as at least potentially of the same virtue
as the ancient, and they applied to themselves the principles by which the masters were judged, made on themselves the same demands as they made on the ancients.
The French, and after them the English, had defended
their mother tongues on the ground of possibilities, not
of accomplishment ; they had to prove those possibilities
by their own endeavours.   To stand beside the learned
poets of the ancient world required learning.   A scholarly
and philosophic poetry can be made only by scholars and
philosophers ; and in any case these men loved learning.
' Certainly it were too easy a thing, and indeed con-
temptible, to make oneself eternal by fame, if the happi-
ness of nature given to the most ignorant were sufficient
to make a matter worthy of immortality.   Whoso wishes
to take flight in the hands and mouths of men, must tarry
long in his chamber : and whoso desires to live in the
memory of posterity must, as one dead to himself, sweat
and tremble oftentimes, and . . . endure hunger, thirst,
and long vigils.   These are the wings by which the
writings of men fly to heaven.'[2]   So also Harvey : ' It
is not sufficient for poets, to be superficial humanists :
but they must be exquisite artists, and curious universal

---

[1] Gabriel Harvey's *Marginalia*, ed. G. C. Moore Smith.
[2] Du Bellay, *Deff. et Ill.*, p. 110.

schollers.'[1] For the Pléiade, the great enemy was
ignorance, and so it was for Spenser. The curiously
unprophetic *Teares of the Muses* would be evidence
enough, even if every page he wrote did not bear the
print of scholarship. His poetry, though ' not to be
gotten by labour and learning,' is ' adorned by both.'[2]
. Learning, in the minds of men of humanist training,
carried with it the theory of imitation. The age pulsed
with new life, yet was but half emancipated from authority. The new poets could not but imitate ; it was enjoined by all their masters, and they applied the method
of their schooldays to the labours of their maturity. But
they regarded the precedents with a fresh eye, drew their
own conclusions, and found authority enough for their
undertaking. Cicero and Virgil appeared to them no
longer as the archetypes of prose and verse, but as men
who in their time had shown how to set about improving
a homely literature by the importation of good methods
and fine models. ' That people of *Rome* having platted
their government, much what like the *Athenian*, for their
common pleas, became enamoured with their eloquence,
whose use theie stood in nede of, and translated their
learning, where with theie were in love. . . . I confesse
their furniture and wish it were in ours, which was taken
from other, to furnish out them. For the tungs which
we study, were not the first getters, tho by learned travell
theie prove good keepers, and yet readily to return and
discharge their trust, when it shall be demanded in such
a sort, as was committed for a term of years, and not for
inheritance.'[3]

---

[1] *Marginalia, ut sup.*
[2] *The Shepheardes Calender*, Argument to *October*.
[3] Mulcaster, *Elementarie*, p. 253. Cf. du Bellay, p. 69 ff.

Mulcaster accepts completely the modernist position, that the ancient tongues have had their day and that it is now the day of the new. He is prepared to defend his position against both humanist superciliousness and the inertness of mind that masks as native simplicity ; and it is Cicero he quotes for his authority. ' But ye will say (the English tongue) is uncouth. In dede being unused. And so was it in Latin, and so is it in ech language, and *Tullie* himself the *Romane* paragon, while he was alive, and our best pattern now, tho he be dead, had verie much ado, and verie great wrastling against such wranglers, and their nice lothing of their naturall speche.' [1] ' Doth anie man of judgement in learning, and the *Latin* tung, think that *Tullies* orations and his discourses in philosophie, were of like known, or of like planesse to the peple of Rome, tho either in their kinde, were allwaie like plane, as theie be to us, which know the *Latin* tung better than our own, bycause we pore upon it, and never mark our own ? No sure. To them theie were not, as it doth appear by verie manie places in *Tullie* himself, where he noteth the difference, and confesseth himself that the newnesse of those argu-ments, which he transported from Grece, were cause of som darknesse to his common reader, and of som contempt to them, that were cunning, bycause of the Greke which they fantsied more. . . . And this was not onelie for the matter, which he wrote of, but also for the maner, which he used in writing, naie even for the words, which the common man knew not, being artificiall and strange as he himself witnesseth.' [2]

Thus in his boyhood Spenser learned the theory of

[1] P. 255. Cf. du Bellay, p. 158.
[2] P. 254.

the new poetry : to cultivate the mother tongue by the
importation of the best learning and the imitation of the
best models, wherever these were to be found. The
Italians saw that the Romans had drawn from the Greeks ;
the French, that the Italians had drawn from Greeks
and Romans ; the English, that the French had drawn
from Greeks, Romans, and Italians. And Cicero quoted
old Cato ; there were traces of Ennius as well as of
Homer in the works of Virgil, of the troubadours and
romancers in Petrarch and Ariosto. Ronsard referred
the pupil of *l'Art Poétique* to old French poets as models
of verse, copied Marot as well as Pindar in his *Odes*, and
took the subject of his heroic poem from Jean Lemaire.
Spenser studied the classics and took Chaucer as his
master of language.

The contribution of the humanists, then, was the nobler
theory of literature and the provision of the models.
Models, however, are not enough by themselves : there
must be guidance and support, and this also they provided.
The naïve and pedantic ' Receipts to form an Epic Poem '
have been sufficiently discredited and derided, but it is
arguable that they were what the time required. Criticism, of course, never made a poet, but in a happy moment
the critic may make up the poet's mind for him, crystallize
his thought about his art, even if only by opposition, and,
with all its faults, humanist criticism was intended to help
poets to write poetry. The modern poet may scoff at it ;
Ariosto, Ronsard, Spenser, Milton, heeded its lessons.
Weaklings may have submitted to ' rules ' because Aristotle dictated them, and been broken in the process.
But that is no reason why the strong man, finding that
Aristotle said some very sensible things about poetry,
should not incorporate them in his own canon. Aris-

totle formulated clearly and finally certain principles : he formulated them, but it is the poet himself who recognizes their validity, and in his freedom accepts them.

In the formation of Spenser's poetic art personal instinct, the tradition of the past, and the fashion of the moment operated no less powerfully than with any other poet, but it is one of the marks of the new poetry that the presence of a reasoned critical basis is immediately perceptible, and this critical basis was laid down at school and in the University, on humanist lines. Explicit discussion of the foundations of literature, in Greek and Latin, would form part of the ordinary course of study, along with the less philosophical but almost more important work of the grammarians and rhetoricians who concentrate attention on form and style, and the commentators who explain and compare points of detail. Modern scholars added to the mass, arguing on the nature and origin of poetry, its value and dignity, on its forms and its methods, analysing and re-analysing the works of the masters. For the aim of the classicist critic is not the expression of personal taste or the exposition of a theory of psychology. ' Here,' he says, ' is poetry which every one acknowledges to be great poetry. How did the poet do it ? ' Beginning, for instance, with the hypothesis that there are distinct ' kinds ' in literature—tragedy, comedy, epic, and so on—he proceeds to isolate from the best examples the character and conditions of the kinds, as norms for judgment and scaffoldings for new construction.

Spenser inherited all this mass of theory and comment, and with it the habit of it. He would be taught to examine works of poetic art under the heads of Invention, Disposition, and Elocution, to study the treatment of Episodes, Recognitions, Descriptions, Supernatural Machinery, and the devising of pithy Aphorisms. And he would be taught to plan and to examine his own work in the same manner, by his teachers, and by the French and Italian critics who, more or less trained in the classical schools, professing classical principles drawn from the practice of Virgil and the precept of Horace, had applied the humanist system to vernacular poetry. Such a training was bound to make a young poet deliberate and self-conscious : the poet who is to found a new school of poetry has to be deliberate and self-conscious. A critical system which consists largely of the abstraction of the practice of Homer and Virgil may be a lending of the armour of Saul, but Spenser had the strength along with the courage to assume it.

In any case he did not attempt, any more than Ariosto or Ronsard, to comply with all the precepts of all the critics or with all the precepts of any one critic. Instinct and tradition and fashion operate in critical thought as well as in creative imagination, and Spenser would be guided by them, as well as by reason and example, in selecting the ideas and methods which might be useful to him in his work. Thus, though the subject of *The Faerie Queene* was condemned in advance by Ascham, at the time by Harvey, though on the important question of diction he traversed opinion which might be expected to weigh with him—from that of Sir John Cheke, the founder of Cambridge humanism, to his patron Sidney's—he persisted in his own way, for he had other authority to show for all he did.

So we find him setting out, with an academic solemnity which it would be crude to call pedantic and stupid to dislike—setting out not only a disciple, but challenging, to prove his mother tongue capable and himself a master.

CHAPTER II

The Kinds of Poetry

The Shepheardes Calender was not Spenser's first essay
in poetry, though, with the exception of the unrhymed
translations in van der Noodt's *Theatre*, it was his first
publication. His friend and commentator, E.K., mentions 'divers other excellent works of his, which slepe
in silence, as his *Dreams*, his *Legendes*, his *Court of Cupide*,
and sondry others.' Why did he choose to appear before
the world with this rather than another? The first
book of a new poet is either an experiment, or a manifesto,
or a declaration of allegiance to a school; *The Shepheardes
Calender* partakes of the nature of all three. It was
obviously experimental, if by no other token than its
unprecedented variety of style, verse, and matter ; it
proclaimed the inauguration of a new way of writing ;
and it showed whence that new way of writing was derived.
The book is the work of an immature poet : on the other
hand it is no boyish firework, but the first issue of a formed
theory, already thought out and written down in that
English Poet which E.K. so unfortunately did not publish.[1]
The Shepheardes Calender could be placed. Nothing like
it had appeared in England before, but it was made after
a recognizable and respectable form.

The new English poet, natural heir to Chaucer and
heir by culture to Virgil, had the precedent example of

[1] See the Argument to *October*.

34

ancient and modern poetry, and the guidance of ancient and modern theory and commentary. When *The Shepheardes Calender* was published he was some twenty-seven years of age—and it was a time when men grew quickly to maturity—had passed under the ferula of a notable schoolmaster, had resided in Cambridge his four years for Bachelor of Arts and three for Master, and had served for about three years an active bishop and a still more active politician. Spenser was very conscious that he was attempting something new, but he had in mind quite definitely what that new thing was and was at some pains to make it clear—rather than leave it to chance and the reader he followed the example of Ronsard and procured a friend to introduce and comment on his work. The contribution of E.K. is far removed from the conventional or the profit-seeking Epistle Dedicatory of the time : the only reason for an introduction and notes addressed by their obscure compiler to a rather unpopular don in one of the lesser colleges of Cambridge is that they were considered necessary. Such apparatus had long been included in editions of the classics, because ancient matters and obsolete languages required explanation, and, for somewhat similar reasons, in editions of Dante and Petrarch. Now it is attached to new work, to prepare the reader's mind for novelty, and to forestall criticism.[1] So E.K. sedulously quotes imitations and parallels, remarks on figures of speech, glosses unusual words, and hints at facts and personalities veiled by the poet. It is part of his function to point out, lest it pass unnoticed by the reader, that his shy and self-conscious friend is following the best precedents, classical, foreign,

---

[1] Compare Muret's commentary to Ronsard's *Amours,* and his introductory epistle.

and English.   Deriving his poet from Virgil, Mantuan,
and Chaucer, he canvasses for the support of both humanist and nationalist.   Spenser, in short, opens his career
with the work which will most definitely declare his position and place him in his proper light before the eyes
of England.

The journey to Parnassus is always an adventure, but
this pilgrim at least was setting out by the well-estab-
lished road, the road by which many distinguished predecessors had arrived.   Of all the classical 'kinds,'
Pastoral was, since Virgil set the example, the one proper
to the young poet.   Vida, the sacred bard of imitative
humanism, had said it :

> But in no Iliad let the youth engage
> His tender years and inexperienced age ;
> Let him by just degrees and steps proceed,
> Sing with the swains, and tune the tender reed.[1]

E.K. states the position exactly : ' And also appeareth
by the baseness of the name, wherein, it semeth, he chose
rather to unfold great matter of argument covertly, then
professing it, not suffice thereto accordingly.   Which
moved him rather in Æglogues, then other wise to write,
doubting perhaps his habilitie, which he little needed,
or mynding to furnish our tongue, with this kinde,
wherein it faulteth, or following the example of the best
and most auncient Poetes, which devised this kind of
wryting, being both so base for the matter, and homely
for the manner, at the first to trye theyr habilities : and
as young birdes, that be newly crept out of the nest, by
little first to prove theyr tender wyngs, before they make
a greater flyght.   So flew Theocritus, as you may perceive he was all ready full fledged.   So flew Virgile, as

---

[1] Vida, *Ars Poetica*, I, 459–461.   Christopher Pitt's translation.

not yet well feeling his winges. So flew Mantuane, as being not full somd. So Petrarque. So Boccace. So Marot, Sanazarus, and also divers other excellent both Italian and French Poetes, whose foting this Author every where followeth, yet so as few, but they be well sented, can trace him out. So finally flyeth this our new Poete, as a bird, whose principals be scarce growen out, but yet as that in time shall be hable to keepe wing with the best.'[1]

E.K. gives a choice of motives, well knowing that all of them would apply. The enrichment of England by increase in her store of poetry was in many men's minds. Roger Ascham had said—if an authoritative English name was required—that the careful selection and imitation of a good model was ' not only to serve in the *Latin* and *Greke* tong, but also in our own English language. But yet, bicause the providence of God hath left unto us in no other tong, save onelie in the *Greke* and *Latin* tong, the trew preceptes and perfite examples of eloquence, therefore must we seeke in the Authors onelie of these two tonges the trewe Paterne of Eloquence, if in any other mother tongue we looke to attaine either to perfit utterance of it ourselves or skilfull judgement of it in others.' [2] This remark of Ascham's was, however, only a suggestion in passing, surrounded with difficulties, and made sterile by the humanist exclusiveness which relegated to the vernacular only the humblest and meanest of tasks, or condescended upon it when it was necessary to address the unlearned. To Ascham the meeting of Chaucer and Virgil meant conflict—to Spenser, reconciliation. Having observed how other lands had accom-

---

[1] Introduction to *Shep. Cal.*
[2] *Scholemaster*, ed. Arber, p. 138.

plished the unification of ancient and modern thought and art, Spencer was doing it for England. The presence of the commentary in his book itself implied that he was engaged on no casual pastime, but on a serious labour, worthy of careful and detailed study ; and there are two implications in the excerpt from E.K.'s introduction quoted above, both of them inconsistent with the humility attributed to the young poet : that he has ' great matter of argument ' to unfold, and that these eclogues are but preparatory to a higher flight.

It is scarcely necessary to recall once more the history of the artificial pastoral, how Virgil made the rural song, already conventionalized by the school of Alexandria, the vehicle of personal opinion, and how his Renaissance imitators took over that usage from him, along with the decorative scheme and its formulas. The convention as Spenser would learn it does not mean merely that the poet should write about shepherds, but that, writing about shepherds, he was at liberty to write about himself and his friends. The reverence of the Renaissance for precedent, for poetic ' good form,' seems to leave the poet little scope for the direct utterance of personal moods and ideas. The habit of mind that regarded the poet as an artificer, the theory of the poet as teacher, and the proud assumption of divine inspiration alike appear to forbid his appearance in public in his own person. Self-revelation was not yet a virtue, still less a touchstone of excellence ; and indeed the greater poets of the time seem to have been too absorbed in life—in writing poetry, for instance—to spend much time or care on cultivating and observing their personalities. ' The subject of good poets,' said Ronsard, ' is fable and fiction.' [1]

---

[1] *Art Poétique*, p. 285.

This is not to say that Renaissance poetry was mechanical. Personality can express itself in any terms if it be powerful enough, and it is a proof of strength that the new poets had assimilated the work of their predecessors so completely that they were able to express themselves in terms, part of whose recommendation was that they had been used before. In any case, Spenser accepted the convention, and even loved it. The term ' shepherd ' had come to mean ' poet,' and, by its reminiscence of Virgil, ' scholar-poet ' : that was Spenser's chosen profession, and the pastoral episode in the Sixth Book of *The Faerie Queene* suggests that the symbols of rural quiet and simplicity express an inward desire—the same desire that dictated the wistful sonnet to Harvey. Throughout his life, whenever Spenser speaks of himself, it is as the Shepherd Colin. The publication of *The Shepheardes Calender*, then, meant the enrichment of English poetry not only through the naturalization of a new poetic form, but by the advent of a new poetic personality.

In *The Shepheardes Calender* Spenser declared himself. Even discounting his own hints and without the aid of the commentary, the group of cultured friends to whom the poems were in the first instance addressed would understand his critical position and recognize his literary affiliation. And they would recognize more than literary interests and affinities : this was a modern work, about living people and contemporary affairs, and stating opinions upon some of them. Under Elizabeth and her ministers the statement of views upon political and ecclesiastical matters was not a welcome or even a safe employment. In that despotic sixteenth century, in any Western country, controversy was unwise, especially, as Marot had found, for poets, who live by favour. It was possible for a man of established position like Ronsard to address his sovereign in solemn Discourses. To a reckless fighter like d'Aubigny *Les Tragiques* could add only a trifling risk to those he faced daily with grim enjoyment. It was another matter for a young man who, as we learn from his letters, was proposing to carve out a career for himself with poetry for his weapon, and had a taste for the peaceful pursuits of scholarship. Yet Spenser did it. If poetry was as important to the world as the new poets claimed, it had to prove its importance by treating of the interests and difficulties of the world, and influencing the minds of men for good. And because Spenser, as a real poet and not as a mere decorator or purveyor of facile pleasure, wished to play his part among the dangers and difficulties of the world, he adopted a form to cover his boldness. The precedents of Virgil and Mantuan could be cited as giving authority for the poet's hardihood, and even as calling for it.[1] Thus all his motives point in the same direction : which is one of the marks of a strong mind.

It was eleven years before another work of this our New Poet appeared in print. Manuscripts were passing from hand to hand, as was usual at the time—this we know from Ponsonby the publisher's preface to the *Complaints*—but Spenser gave to none of them, as yet, the dignity and permanence of type. He had his greater purpose to serve, his promise of the higher flight to

---

[1] Thus similar interests emerge naturally in *Lycidas*, a growth of the same tree. When the young Milton wrote directly about his own affairs and projects, he in his turn adopted the recognized conventions, and added the further artificiality of Latin.

fulfil. By all the rules of the game, that higher flight
meant Tragedy or Heroic Poetry.

> Abandon then the base and viler clowne,
> Lyft up thy selfe out of the lowly dust :
> And sing of bloody Mars, of wars, of giusts,
> Turne thee to those, that weld the awful crowne,
> To doubted Knights, whose woundless armour rusts,
> And helmes unbruzed wexen dayly browne.

> There may thy Muse display her fluttryng wing,
> And stretch her selfe at large from East to West . . .

> O if my temples were distaind with wine,
> And girt in garlonds of wild Yvie twine,
> How I could reare the Muse on stately stage,
> And teache her tread aloft in bus-kin fine,
> With queint *Bellona* in her equipage.[1]

There is an element of drama in *The Shepheardes
Calender*, for the figure of the Shepheard Colin is presented, an assumed character, but an individual one, and
surrounded by others whose relations to the central
figure make the technical form of the pastoral ; part of
the strength and appeal of the book, indeed, is in the
solidity gained by referring the poet's sentiments to a
named and distinguishable figure. Spenser's one dramatic project, however, was evidently short-lived, for it
appears only in one of Harvey's letters, and there as
already abandoned in favour of the Heroic Poem.[2]
Why the *Nine Comedies* were abandoned no man can
tell, nor whether they would have had any effect on the
course of English drama. Of all forms of literature,

---

[1] *Shep. Cal.*, Oct., 37–44, 110–114.
[2] *Elizabethan Critical Essays*, I, 115.

4

drama is most dependent on social conditions and technical apparatus, and, if we may judge from Harvey's
remarks, the inspiration of Spenser's comedies was
entirely literary. John Lyly, whose *Euphues* appeared
in the same year as *The Shepheardes Calender*, and who
had had the same kind of training in Oxford as Spenser
in Cambridge, set the mode of English comedy, but
fortune, by placing him in the Office of the Revels, gave
him the opportunity, even made it his business, to exploit
his literary gifts and training in that end. ' You know,'
wrote Harvey, admonishing Spenser to persevere with
the Nine Comedies, ' it hath bene the usual practise of
the most exquisite and odde wittes in all nations, and
specially in *Italie*, rather to shewe and advaunce themselves that way than any other : as, namely, those three
notorious dyscoursing heads, Bibiena, Machiavel, and
Aretine did (to let Bembo and Ariosto passe) with the
great admiration and wonderment of the whole coun-
trey ' [1]; but the enmity of Burleigh made it impossible
for Spenser to thrive at court, and comedy is not a plant
of the desert, even if Spenser had possessed—as he did
not—the fanciful humour of Lyly or the hard intellectual
wit of Ariosto and Machiavelli. In 1580, the year of
Harvey's letter, the theatre within which a young man
might make a career was not yet built, and when it was
being built, and Spenser's own pupils were gathering
round it to found the English drama, Spenser was in
Ireland.

For entirely practical reasons, tragedy was another
man's destiny, and in any case there were literary reasons
—the only kind which at that date could seriously affect
his decision—why he should attempt the Heroic Poem

[1] *Ibid.,* 116.

rather than Tragedy. Humanist thought centred round Virgil. Greek tragedy was comparatively unknown and little understood, and the tragedies of Seneca were so obviously inferior to the epic of Virgil that critical attention was inevitably directed on the latter. The new poets whose ideals were taken from the humanists naturally accepted the Heroic as the form for their masterpieces, and among the younger Italian critics the tendency to concentrate on it was accentuated by the fact that the new poetry in Italy really began with a Heroic Poem, Ariosto's *Orlando Furioso,* while, in spite of many well-meant efforts, no one had succeeded in acclimatizing the classical tragedy. Italian tragedy was too purely literary and classical, an affair of the critics—Trissino, Giraldi Cinthio, Speroni—and the French imitation was as weak, until Corneille, a practical man of the theatre working for a mixed audience, infused some stronger Spanish blood into it. English tragedy, of course, was frankly barbarian and professional, and it is as well that Spenser did not develop into an earlier Sir William Alexander. Instead, he found the Italians adapting the principles of Tragedy, as set forth by Aristotle, to Epic.

Italian criticism of Ariosto was largely concerned with defining the form of *Orlando Furioso* and relating it to epic, and especially to the *Æneid.* There were obvious borrowings and imitations to point out—with his humanist training Ariosto could scarcely have avoided indebtedness to Virgil—but the loose and casual conduct of his story, the division into *canti* instead of into Books, the addresses to an audience at the opening of each Canto, the status of the characters, all had to be discussed and justified. The final position of the critics Geraldi

Cinthio and Giambattista Pigna [1] was much like that of Dryden in regard to Shakespeare : this was not the form as Aristotle had defined it, but it had so much in common, and was so undeniably good of its kind, that had Aristotle known it he might have extended his definition to include it. They proceeded to do for Ariostian Romance what other critics did for Virgilian Epic—to disengage its characteristics, explain its method, and point out its value, constantly setting it alongside epic for comparison, and identifying the two wherever possible.

Before Giraldi and Pigna had published their studies of Ariosto, however, the Heroic character of *Orlando Furioso* had been noticed by du Bellay. His desire to have France set in equality with Greece and Rome was augmented by a proper jealousy of Italy and her more recent achievement. ' If thou hast at times pity on thy poor language, if thou deignest to enrich her with thy treasures, it will be thou in truth that wilt make her lift up her head, and with a brave brow even herself to the proud Greek and Roman tongues, as has done in our time, in his own vernacular, the Italian Ariosto, whom I would dare, but for the sacredness of the ancient poems, to compare to Homer and Virgil.' [2] The distinction between Romance and Epic does not seem to have occurred to the French poets : du Bellay heads his chapter on the subject simply ' Of the Long Poem.' Unlike the Italians, they had no incentive to attempt the justification of Ariosto, and when Ronsard faced the mighty

---

[1] G.-B. Giraldi Cinthio, *Discorsi dei Romanzi*, and G.-B. Pigna, *I Romanzi*, both published 1554. Their conclusions are very similar, and each accused the other of plagiarism.

[2] *Deff. et Ill.*, p. 119.

task in *La Franciade*, he attacked the weakness of *Orlando Furioso*, ' the members of which are extremely beautiful, but the body so misshapen and monstrous that it is more like the dreams of one sick of a continued fever than the inventions of a healthy man.'[1] To remedy this failure of construction Ronsard attempted strict adherence to the epic formula as laid down by Minturno,[2] which cramped his efforts and ruined his poem. So far as the kind is concerned, he makes no distinction ; it is a question of treatment, of ' disposition.' Historical criticism was not yet, and the men of the Renaissance saw and felt simply. To them the *Iliad* was a poem that a man had written, not the product of a certain stage of human civilization ; the *Æneid* was another. Nor were they troubled by the division of literature into the classics and the others : their whole position was a denial of such division. They imitated their elder brethren of Greece and Rome rather than those of mediaeval France, because the Greeks and Romans had written much the better poetry. So Ronsard, having prefixed the formidable quatrain :

> Les François qui ces vers liront,
> S'ils ne sont et Grecs et Romains,
> En lieu de mon livre ils n'auront
> Qu'un pesant faix entre les mains,

introduces La Franciade with the perfectly just remark, ' This poem is a Romance like the Iliad and the Æneid.'

In the same fashion Spenser quotes as his precedents Homer, Virgil, Ariosto, and Tasso, and the only distinction he makes is between their supposed didactic

---

[1] Preface to *La Franciade*.
[2] *De Poeta*, 1559, also *L'Arte Poetica*, 1563.

purposes : ' I have followed all the antique Poets his-
toricall, first Homere, who in the Persons of Agamemnon
and Ulysses hath ensampled a good governour and a
vertuous man . . . then Virgil, whose like intention was
to doe in the person of Æneas : after him Ariosto com-
prised them both in his Orlando : and lately Tasso dis-
severed them again, and formed both parts in two persons.'[1] Thus he is close to the position of du Bellay,
which may well have been his starting-point, though
this young man who worked so seriously at his business
of poetry must have known the Italian critics of a poet
he strove to ' overgo,' and was, of course, versed in the
rules of the humanists. The form of *The Faerie Queene*
has been attacked and defended, but, successful or not,
it cannot be held to have been fortuitous. Spenser was
working under difficult conditions—it is not easy to
maintain unity or even connexion throughout a long and
complicated piece of literary work when one's real working day is occupied by legal and administrative duties,
varied with occasional fighting—he may not have been
very certain of his design, and may have changed his
mind as the work progressed, but he must have thought
about it, the theory of the Kinds must have been the basis
of his thinking, and the relation of Romance and Epic
must have been the subject of his careful consideration.
And, since both had strong claims upon his regard, he
attempted to follow both.

The Faerie Queene is an attempt to reconcile the old
native virtues and the new literary demands, and, as has
been suggested, the reconciliation was not so difficult as
might appear to a modern mind, sophisticated by generations of criticism in which the opposition of Romantic

[1] Letter to Sir Walter Raleigh, appended to *The Faerie Queene*.

and Classic has been a commonplace. Ariosto, says
Pigna, ' turning to Tuscan poetry . . . took as his object
Romantic composition, holding such composition as
similar to Heroic and Epic.'[1] Giraldi Cinthio has the
same notion : ' I let myself be easily persuaded that
this custom of composing romances has arisen among us
in place of the heroic compositions of the Greeks and
Latins. For just as the latter wrote in their tongues the
illustrious and eminent deeds of powerful knights, so
those who have given themselves to the writing of
romances treat of fictitious matters of knights whom
they call knights errant. Hence are seen in their compositions virtuous and courageous deeds, mingled with
loves, with courtesies, with games, with strange happenings, as the Greeks and Latins did in their compositions.'[2]
Minturno alludes somewhat contemptuously to this
opinion, for in his narrow-minded classicism he despises
all that is derived from the barbarians,[3] but French and
English poets might well attempt to show that the ' barbarian ' matter, which was their own and their country's,
could be wrought into a great form.

Du Bellay calls on the patriotic scholar-poet : ' Like
Ariosto . . . choose me some one of those fine old French
romances, such as Lancelot, Tristan, and so on, and from
it make to be born into the world again an admirable
Iliad and laborious Æneid.'[4] Ronsard founds *La
Franciade* on the example of Homer, who wrote on the
Trojan War, ' since the report of such a war was received
in the common opinion of the men of that time,' and on
that of Virgil, ' who, reading in Homer that Æneas
should not die in the Trojan War and that his descendants

[1] *I Romanzi*, p. 74.   [2] *Discorsi*, p. 5.
[3] *L'Arte Poetica*, p. 27 ff.   [4] *Deff. et Ill.*, p. 120.

should uplift the Phrygian name again, and seeing that the ancient annals of his time said that Æneas had founded the city of Alba which was afterwards Rome . . . conceived that divine Æneid.'¹   He made it clearer in his later draft of this preface, which was printed long after *The Faerie Queene* was planned and begun, but which is valuable as an indication of the general movement, the more that it is addressed to 'The Apprentice Reader.'   'The good poet lays the foundation of his work on some old annals of the past, or long-established report which has gained credit in the minds of men ; as Virgil on the common report that a certain Trojan named Æneas, sung by Homer, came to the Lavinian shores. . . . On such opinion already received by the people he built his book of the Æneid.   Homer before him had done the same, who coming across some old tale of his time about the fair Helen and the army of the Greeks at Troy, as we do tales of Lancelot, of Tristan, of Gawain and Arthur, founded thereon his Iliad.'²   Thus Spenser, choosing the history of King Arthur, was not departing from the epic.   On the other hand, it will be noted that Giraldi speaks of the matter of Romance as fictitious, so that in choosing to sing of Arthur's adventures before he became king and in inventing his knights, he was following the method of Romance.

In the letter to Raleigh which he wisely printed with the first three Books of *The Faerie Queene* Spenser refrains from lengthy critical dissertation, but he says enough to show how it is all based on critical theory. ' I chose the historye of king Arthure, as most fitte for the excellence of his person, being made famous by many mens former workes.'   This may be compared

¹ First Preface, p. 9.   ² Preface of 1587, p. 23.

with Pigna's explanation of Ariosto's choosing to continue the story of Boiardo's *Orlando Innamorato*, ' perhaps because he knew that his *Innamoramento* was very finely planned, or perhaps so as not to introduce new names of persons and new beginnings of matter to the ears of the Italians, since the subjects of the Count [Boiardo] were already impressed and established in their minds to such an extent that if he did not continue it, but began a different story, he would have composed a thing little delightful. In the same way Virgil did not depart from the poetry of Homer, since it was already accepted by all and confirmed in all, so that everything unlike it would have been despised by all as unpoetical.'[1] Virgil continued the work of Homer, Ariosto that of Boiardo ; Spenser could not continue the story of Arthur, because it was already closed with his death, so he invented earlier history than that of Malory, ' also furthest from the daunger of envy, and suspition of present time.' In his *Abrégé de l'Art Poétique* Ronsard had said, ' Thou shalt never begin the discourse of a great poem unless it be removed from the memory of men,' but this is apparently to give purpose to the usual invocation of the Muse, ' who being a goddess remembers all things '[2] ; Spenser's reason for choosing a far-away subject may have some connexion with another epic commonplace in which he was particularly concerned, the political allegory and contemporary allusions in his poem, and especially its praise of Queen Elizabeth.

According to Pigna, when Ariosto ' had first given himself to the court of the Cardinal da Este, he wished, in order to exalt him the more, to celebrate all his house-hold together, just as Virgil did, who speaks of the other

---

[1] *I Romanzi*, p. 75.   [2] P. 324.

Romans on account of Augustus.'[1] ' It will not be accounted a fault also if we point to something done in our own days, as Æneas in the presence of Dido at his parting is an allusion to Augustus, who lowered his eyes at the sight of Cleopatra, not to be inflamed by her ; and the death of Anchises, with the games made for him, to Julius Cæsar, and to the same, Venulus hurled from his saddle by Tarchon ; and Antone which should be read instead of Antore, to Antony, when he died ; and Lausus to Scipio, when he gave his own life for his father, who would have been killed. To which Ariosto conformed in many places, which are transparent from his own explanation to those who conversed with him.'[2] So also Ronsard : ' Homer . . . wishing to insinuate himself into the favour of the Æacides . . . engaged on a poem so divine and perfect to make himself and the Æacides together much honoured for ever by his labour. . . . As much must be thought of Virgil, who . . . in order to gain the goodwill of the Cæsars . . . conceived that divine Æneid.'[3] It is unnecessary to quote from Spenser to show how strong this motive is in all his work.

Thus in choosing the national legend of Arthur, and in using it to shadow events of his own time, Spenser was acting on recognized principles : Homer, Virgil, Ariosto, Ronsard, had done so before him. The choice of matter suited the national feeling—Boiardo probably took up the Charlemagne cycle because it fell under his hand, though indeed Italy had a hereditary interest in Emperors, and in Charlemagne himself—the Matter of Britain was inevitable to Spenser, and it could be defended upon the best classical precedents. Milton and Dryden, who both meditated the same scheme, would have given

[1] *I Romanzi*, p. 76. [2] P. 92. [3] First Preface to *La Franciade*, p. 9.

the same reasons. He appears to have attempted
another combination of methods. Giraldi Cinthio distinguishes between Epic and Romance again thus :
' The subjects or materials of the romances are not after
the same manner as those of Virgil and of Homer. For
each of the latter have set themselves in their compositions
to imitate a single action of a single man, and ours have
many actions, not only of one man, but of many. For
the fabric of their work is built up on eight or ten
people.' [1] Pigna, who compares Romance more closely
with Epic, varies this statement slightly : ' In order
to be Epic, this illustrious action shall be one single
action of one single person. . . . The Romances set
themselves indeed to many actions of many men, but
propose to themselves one man especially, who is celebrated above all the others, and so they concur with the
Epics in choosing a single person, but as to a single
event it is not so, for they treat of as many as they think
enough.' [2] When *The Faerie Queene* is examined in
this light, it is evident that Spenser had the virtues of
both in view, and even if his difficulties are partly solved
by Pigna's pre-eminent hero, he inclines to the method
which, of several discussed by Pigna, is nearest to Epic.
The Faerie Queene treats of many actions of many men,
but there is an attempt to give it unity by interweaving
with these actions the single epic action of the single epic
hero, Prince Arthur's search for Gloriana. The attempt
is not successful, but it is made, and the device of separ-
ating the minor actions into Books may be an attempt
to keep the minor heroes in their places, so that the
greater action and the greater hero may be more clearly
disengaged and ensured his due share of attention.

[1] P. 11.   [2] P. 25. Cf. Minturno, *L'Arte Poetica*, p. 27.

The story of Arthegall and Britomart succeeds in overriding the division between Books III and IV, just as that of Ruggiero and Bradamante, from which Spenser's story was imitated, thrusts into the background the principal action of the madness of Orlando, and for the same reasons, that its bearing on contemporary events and ' le los du seigneur ' gave it an undesigned prominence, and that the main action was not completely clear in all its bearings even to the poet himself. The coincidence of the Twelve Paladins and the Twelve Books of the Æneid probably had more to do with the original plan of *The Faerie Queene* than any ' invention ' or ' disposition ' of the tale of Prince Arthur.

The incompleteness of *The Faerie Queene* obscures the construction more than incompleteness need, because the over-ingenious scheme did not grow out of the main action, or out of any action, but was devised from purely mechanical data of critical theory, and especially, as Spenser himself had to confess, because of that constantly cited commonplace of Epic criticism, ' to begin in the middle,' derived from Horace.

> Nor does he run his subject out of breath
> In dry detail from Meleager's death
> To Diomed's return ; nor yet begins
> The Trojan War from Leda and her twins ;
> But posting onwards, brooking no delay,
> To the mid-theme he boldly bursts his way.
> Much he anticipates as if 'twere known ;
> Much that he feels would tire he lets alone ;
> And so adroitly mingles false with true,
> So with his fair illusions cheats the view,
> That all the parts, beginning, middle, end,
> In one harmonious compound sweetly blend.[1]

---

[1] *Ars Poetica*, 146–152. Howes's translation.

Pigna notes that ' Nowadays this is in everyone's mouth, that one should not begin *ab ovo*.' [1] Each Book of *The Faerie Queene* is constructed upon this principle of ' disposition,' and so is the poem as a whole, and it is the latter that makes the explanation necessary. ' The methode of a Poet historical is not such, as of an Historiographer. For an Historiographer discourseth of affayres orderly as they were done, accounting as well the times as the actions, but a Poet thrusteth into the middest, even where it most concerneth him, and there recoursing to thinges forepaste, and divining of thinges to come, maketh a pleasing Analysis of all.' [2] The contrast of poet and historian is made by Pigna, by Giraldi Cinthio, by Minturno, and most clearly by Ronsard ; Spenser could hardly escape it, and his statement of the principle suggests that he regarded his poem as having at least some of the nature of Epic. Cinthio remarks that ' there are a thousand ways of shortening the length of the work without ceasing to describe all the life of the hero of whom the poet has set himself to write, as making some things be predicted by seers, making others be painted, and making others be narrated,' [3] all of which expedients Spenser adopted ; but when he leaves the biographical poem Cinthio distinguishes two other kinds of Heroic, the Epic and the Romantic types, each having its appropriate method of disposition. ' First it is to be ascertained, whether it is desired to write a poem of one single action, or of many actions of many men, or all those of a single man. If we wish to select the first, I think it laudable to follow the examples of the writers who have written of that in praiseworthy fashion, on whom Aristotle and Horace founded their doctrines.

[1] *I Romanzi*, p. 36.   [2] Letter to Raleigh.   [3] *Discorsi*, p. 21.

And thus the first thing about which warning has to be given will be, not to begin at the beginning, but with that part which seems to the writer to be most to the purpose . . . as we see Homer did. . . . But because I have not seen in our tongue a poem of this manner of composition which merits praise, I shall not dilate much upon it. . . . If the argument of the work is to be of many and various actions of many and various men, as are the compositions of the romances of our tongue . . . the opening will be born of that thing which is of greatest importance, and from which it appears all the others depend or are born, as we see the Count and Ariosto have done.'[1] The disposition of *The Faerie Queene*, then, is based on epic precedents ; here as in its division into Books and also into Cantos, there seems to be an attempt to combine the virtues of both methods of Heroic Poetry.

This idea of reconciliation was, as we have seen, fundamental to the new poetry. The hope to overgo Ariosto by correcting the weakness of *Orlando Furioso* produced this elaborate scheme based on critical principles, as it produced the similar scheme of Tasso. Since, however, it is in the scheme that the attempt is apparent, and the scheme is as early as 1580, when Gabriel Harvey saw part of the poem,[2] it occurred to Spenser in England at least a year before Tasso's *Gerusalemme Liberata* was published in Italy, seven years before the *Discorsi e Lettere* in which Tasso explained his project, and the influence of Tasso probably tended rather to disturb than to assist. The planning is all very dull and pedantic, but the modern reader must remember that this was the latest criticism

[1] *Discorsi*, p. 27 ff.
[2] *Elizabethan Critical Essays*, I, 115.

of the latest poetry, which was being discussed by every
one who was interested in literature ; it is confused and
sometimes contradictory ; probably it was never very
clear to Spenser. Yet it helped. The very diversity
of Spenser's masters saved him from mere chaos, which
might have resulted from the exclusive imitation of
Ariosto and the other romancers, and from the deadly
rigidity of the purely classicist formulas with which
Ronsard shackled himself in *La Franciade*. Even the
existence of this criticism was useful, for it forced people
to think about such questions as matter and construction.
Sheer poetic strength, of course, gave *The Faerie Queene*
its success, but the greatest strength must be directed in
a definite course. The poet has not yet appeared who
can create an entirely new form on a large scale—Wordsworth tried it, and though, unlike Spenser, he had
leisure to think of nothing else, he accomplished only
the *Prelude* to an impossible immensity.

The Shepheardes Calender and *The Faerie Queene* con-
stitute, in a way, Spenser's life-work : they were planned
each on a critical scheme, as parts of the larger scheme
of a poetical career. Until he had begun to fulfil the
promise of the ' higher flight ' with the first three Books
of *The Faerie Queene* in 1590, he published nothing.
That done, and its success assured, the miscellaneous
Complaints were called for and might be allowed to
appear. Virgil had written slight things in his time—
one of them was here translated, for that matter—and
so, surely, might Spenser, once he was able to proclaim
himself the English Virgil in a proud imitation of the
elder poet's exordium :

Ille ego qui quondam gracili modulatus avena
carmen et egressus silvis vicina coegi
ut quamvis avido parerent arva colono
gratum opus agricolis, at nunc horrentia Martis
arma virumque cano . . .

Lo I the man, whose Muse whilome did maske
As time her taught, in lowly Shepheards weeds,
Am now enforst a far unfitter taske,
For trumpets sterne to chaunge mine Oaten reeds,
And sing of Knights and Ladies gentle deeds . . .

Spenser produced no *Georgics,* unless some such notion
lay behind the topographical poem on the rivers of
England, the *Epithalamion Thamesis* mentioned in his
second letter to Harvey [1] and afterwards recast as Canto
XI of the Fourth Book of *The Faerie Queene.* This
might include many of Virgil's motives. It would,
of course, be informative, intellectual teaching as distinct
from moral or spiritual, but such teaching had the
authority of the master, and topography is as respectable
a study as agriculture. If the mind of Augustan Italy
needed to be attracted to the fields, so was it the duty of
the Englishman, conscious of his nationality in a time of
rising patriotism, to know his England, and the Mar-
riage-Song of Thames could be wrought into a panegyric
of that many-watered land as properly as the *Georgics*
into the praise of Virgil's

Magna parens frugum, Saturnia tellus.

It is no coincidence that the poetical survey of England was carried out by one of Spenser's most devoted
followers, in the more prosaic but no less honourable
Polyolbion.

[1] *Elizabethan Critical Essays,* I, 100.

The *Complaints* are ' minor ' poems in a sense in which the eclogues of *The Shepheardes Calender* are not. Spenser, indeed, parallels himself with Virgil again, rather quaintly, in translating the *Culex*, but that was one of Virgil's slighter things, and deliberately so :

> Now we have playde (Augustus) wantonly,
> Tuning our song unto a tender Muse,
> And like a cobweb weaving slenderly,
> Have onley playde : let thus much then excuse
> This Gnats small Poeme, that th' whole history
> Is but a jest.

Virgils Gnat is one large literary allusion, such as may be found, in briefer space but in immense profusion, on any page of *Euphues* : as Virgil to Augustus on one occasion, so Spenser now stands to Leicester, apologizing for a well-meant indiscretion. In the same kind we might reckon *Muiopotmos*. It is mock-heroic as the *Culex* is mock-elegiac, and it has been interpreted as an allegorical allusion to his own fate at the hands of Burleigh ; yet the lighthearted tone of the poem—most unusual in our sage and serious Spenser—seems to contradict the idea of allegory. *Muiopotmos* is Spenser's most original poem, and that because the ' kind ' is simply that of ' minor poetry,' and allows a freedom impossible in most of his other works. So far as the rest of the volume of *Complaints* is concerned, the question of ' kind ' might be waived ; but since the notion of poetic kinds was inveterate in the literary thinking of the Renaissance, it would be more accurate to say that Spenser, true to his mixed breeding and remembering his ancestry, recognized more than the classical kinds, or, as he showed in *The Faerie Queene*, more species within the

5

kinds than the stricter of his humanist teachers might have approved.

That the *Culex* could be held to legitimize *Mother Hubberds Tale* might be dismissed as special pleading, but such a plea was not impossible at the time : ' Did you never reade that under the persons of beastes many abuses were dissiphered ? Have you not reason to waye that whatsoever Virgil did write of his gnatt or Ovid of his fley was all covertly to declare abuse ? '[1] It would be more courtly to Spenser, however, and probably juster, to put it that when he wrought in the satiric kind he chose a mediaeval and not a classical model. *Mother Hubberds Tale* would be ranked by E.K. with the February eclogue of *The Shepheardes Calender* as something learned from Chaucer, and perhaps more truly, since it is introduced as one of many tales told on a particular occasion :

> In this ill plight, there came to visite mee
> Some friends, who sorie my sad case to see,
> Began to comfort me in chearful wise,
> And meanes of gladsome solace to devise . . .
>
> And sitting all in seates about me round,
> With pleasant tales (fit for that idle stound)
> They cast in course to waste the wearie howres.[2]

What Spenser owed to his classical teachers in this connexion was probably the discretion that left the Tale to stand by itself. With all his admiration for Chaucer, Spenser had found in the romantic epic a better method than that of *The Canterbury Tales*, nor was he tempted

---

[1] Thomas Lodge, *Defence of Poetry*, 1597 : *Elizabethan Critical Essays*, I, 65.

[2] Lines 17–20, 25–27.

here, as Chaucer was in *The Legend of Good Women*, into the mediaeval vice of over-labouring his point. If a mediaeval writer had written *Mother Hubberds Tale*, he would have thought it his duty to write twenty more on the same subject to accompany it : Spenser's good sense told him what to take, and then when to stop—the same good sense that had taught him that there were other masters of satire besides Horace, of whose temper he had little share, and Juvenal and Persius, who declared abuse too nakedly to be safe to copy.

This same volume shows how Spenser learned also from the modern foreign poets. Three of the nine *Complaints* are translations, two from du Bellay, one from Petrarch, and *Visions of the Worlds Vanitie* and parts of *The Ruines of Time* are imitations of these ; the translations might be regarded as studies from the model, the others as original exercises in the same manner. This apocalyptic visionary poem is a purely modern kind, or else the Revelations of St. John are to be included among the models—a suggestion by no means without justification, if a passage of Gabriel Harvey's second letter to Spenser be duly considered.[1] It is certainly not a classical kind. *The Teares of the Muses* also is difficult to place : the excited tone and the parade of scholarship are reminiscent of du Bellay's violent and noisy *Musagnoemachie*, though Spenser bewails a defeat where du Bellay hailed the victory of poetry and learning over ' ugly Barbarisme and brutish Ignorance.' The thing is humanistic as *Mother Hubberds Tale* is Chaucerian ; in kind it might be placed among the Odes of Ronsard —as a bad example.

A rather unhappy experiment in the combination of

[1] *Elizabethan Critical Essays*, I, 114–5.

the new vision-kind with the very ancient kind of elegy did not have quite a fair chance in *The Ruines of Time*. The poem is interesting and valuable for the same reasons as *Antony and Cleopatra* : it contains some of the poet's best work, and some of his worst, and in the looseness and haste of its handling tells us more of the author's habits than better-finished work could. Like all the elegiac kind, it is an ' occasional ' poem ; the reason for its existence was not an artistic but a personal or social reason. That does not necessarily make a poem any the worse, but never was the occasional nature of an elegy more naïvely confessed than in Spenser's dedication to the Countess of Pembroke : ' Yet sithens my late cumming into England, some friends of mine (which might much prevaile with me, and indeede commaund me) knowing with howe straight bandes of duetie I was tied to him [1] : as also bound unto that noble house (of which the chiefe hope then rested in him) have sought to revive them by upbraiding me : for that I have not shewed anie thankefull remembrance towards him or any of them ; but suffer their names to sleep in silence and forgetfulnesse. Whome chieflie to satisfie, or els to avoide that fowle blot of unthankefulnesse, I have conceived this small Poeme, intituled by a generall name of the *worlds Ruines* : yet speciallye intended to the renowming of that noble race, from which both you and he sprong, and to the eternizing of some of the chiefe of them lately deceased.' The motive recurs in the course of the poem, where he refers to one published reproach,[2] and accuses himself of ingratitude.[3]

[1] Sir Philip Sidney.
[2] Lines 435–9 ; cf. Thomas Watson, *Poems*, ed. Arber, pp. 172–3.
[3] Lines 225–238.

This family elegy is well 'intituled by a generall name,' for it is a compilation of workshop fragments. Beginning in the visionary manner like another imitation of du Bellay, it reads for the first 175 lines like a commendatory poem on Camden's *Britannia*, which might quite well be expected of one who was the poet of the antiquarianism of sixteenth-century England, as Parker was its patron and Camden its most active worker. To this there succeeds the elegy on Leicester, a moralizing strain after the manner of the *Mirror for Magistrates*, thoroughly mediaeval in tone and spirit, and thereafter some of the worst and baldest lines Spenser ever wrote lead—through a stanza lacking a principal verb and unrelated in syntax either to the stanza before or the one after [1]—into the very beautiful and feeling passage on Philip Sidney. The poet's train of thought may then have led him, after celebrating the dead poet, to sing of the immortal rewards of poetry, but in the fervour of this admirable confession of faith he forgets both Leicester and Sidney, though he remembers the enemy of poets, Burleigh. So he returns to his first subject, the vision of the Genius of Verulam, and closes in the first manner, with emblematic 'pageants' in the style of Petrarch and du Bellay, the second series of which, symbolizing the death of Sidney, is either an afterthought or else an artistic blunder of greater magnitude than is to be expected of Spenser, for in visions above all things discretion must be observed. A brief *Envoy*, such as might have been appended at any time, dedicates the poem once more to the Countess of Pembroke and to the memory of Sidney, and Spenser's duty was done.

When he was called again to lead with *Astrophel* the

[1] Lines 280–287 ; cf. also line 281 with *Teares*, line 361.

chorus of poetical lamentation for Sidney, the accepted formula of pastoral elegy was his natural resource, and the value of the ' kinds ' is shown by the unity and certainty of that otherwise undistinguished poem as compared with the faulty balance of interests, the uncertainty of tone, and the careless rhetoric of *The Ruines of Time*, whose greater brilliance in some passages scarcely compensates for its structural weakness. Convention would almost prescribe the pastoral form of lament for a brother poet—we owe to that convention, and to Spenser's leadership in adopting it, later and better poems in the same mode—for in *Astrophel* Spenser happily ignored the patron for the poet ; but another pastoral elegy, *Daphnaida*, is a curious sophistication. It has long been noticed that this elegy on the wife of Arthur Gorges is a recension of Chaucer's *Boke of the Duchess Blanche*. *Daphnaida* is the result of *contaminatio* of pastoral allegory and mediaeval symbolism—of Virgil and Chaucer—and though the double imitation is typical of Spenser and his dual allegiance, it is not a very happy result. Spenser may have been trying to bring Chaucer up to date, or it may be that, trying the same process as in *Mother Hubberds Tale*, he chose an unsuitable model ; but *Daphnaida* stands with *Lycidas* among attempts to compensate with ingenuity of craftsmanship for the lack of genuine feeling. The quasi-dramatic convention and the semi-dramatic material taken from Chaucer may have been adopted deliberately in order that something might be written about a lady the poet never knew : what beauty of feeling it holds is purely of the imagination—*lacrimae rerum* or tears for Hecuba. It is not that the borrowing of either matter or manner was a bondage to Spenser, but *Daphnaida* was taskwork, the payment of a social—or for all we know a material—debt.

There need be no complaint that such duties should be laid on Spenser. It was the custom of the time ; that was part of a poet's business, and as a professed poet he would accept it himself quite calmly. Only he would not, one imagines, put such work in the same category as those poems which he wrote for his own sake and for the sake of their kinds, in freedom, such as his longest and best Virgilian pastoral *Colin Clouts Come Home Again*, or the *Fowre Hymnes* in which he introduced into England an ancient form which Ronsard had reconstructed for modern purposes in French, or his own most brilliant invention, the adaptation of the Latin marriage-hymn to the form of the Italian canzone in *Epithalamion* and *Prothalamion*, or even his Anacreontic Epigrams— another Pléiade model—and his following of fashion in the Petrarchan *Amoretti*. The naturalization of recognizable ' kinds ' was the first part of Spenser's special work for English poetry. England needed it, for, as has been already said, the rising power of the new age required direction. Shakespeare got his direction from the technical exigencies of the theatre in which he found employment, and was so far fortunate. The poets of Chaucer's time were directed in their subject by certain social limitations and in their technique by the custom of reading aloud. But the new poets of the sixteenth century wrote for a wider and more variously-interested public, and a reading public ; they required the help of critical theory, and first of all, of this theory of the kinds. Spenser's special work in this direction was, then, considerable both in its intrinsic importance and in its extent : he merely thought of tragedy and comedy, but he

revived the satiric fable, helped the vogue of sonneteer-
ing, improved the elegy, and made his England free of
pastoral, hymn, canzone, ode, and epic.   It was a serious
business, for a serious end, and though pressed in different directions by natural claims and motives, he kept the
balance even between Chaucerism and classicism, misled
neither by patriotic self-satisfaction nor by textbook
rule, but seeing the value of each, and seeing the essential unity of their values.

CHAPTER III

Style and Language

The new idea of the new poets was, that the modern age and the modern tongues were capable of poetry as great in kind as the ancient ; it followed that treatment had to be in accord with conception, that the power of expression both of the language and of the poet had to be cultivated. Narrow-minded classicists declared that the vulgar tongues were insufficient for the expression of deep conceptions and deficient in art : the new generation accepted the task of repairing both deficiencies. Spenser would have that task put before him early, by his admirable schoolmaster. ' Tho no English man for want of that exercise, which the *Roman* had, and the Athenian used in their spacious and great courts, do prove a *Tullie* or like to *Demosthenes*, yet for sooth he maie prove verie comparable to them in his own common weal and the eloquence there. And why not in dede comparable to them in all points thorough out for his naturall tung ? Our brains can bring forth, our conceits will bear life ; our tungs be not tyed, and our labor is our own.'[1] It is more than a possibility, it is a duty : ' Our English is our own, our *Sparta* must be spunged, by the inhabitants that have it, as well as those tungs were by the industrie of their people, which be braved with the most, and brag as the best.'[1]

[1] Mulcaster, *Elementarie*, p. 256.

65

Ronsard, the clearest and most vigorous exponent of the new thought, advocated—and exemplified—the double duty of study of the native tongue itself and of its improvement by the assimilation of foreign virtues ; the same plea is in the very title of du Bellay's treatise, ' the defence and embellishment of the French language.' The thought was in many minds, but they gave it its clearest utterance. ' Whoever were the first who dared to abandon the tongue of the ancients to honour that of their country, were truly good children and citizens not ungrateful, and worthy to be crowned on a public statue and that from age to age men should have perpetual memory of them and their virtues. Not that one must be ignorant of foreign tongues ; I advise you to know them perfectly, and with them, as with an ancient treasure found in the earth, to enrich your own nation ; for it is very difficult to write well in the vulgar tongue if one is not learned in those of the most honourable and famous foreigners.' This passage from Ronsard's *Abrégé de l'Art Poétique* occurs under the heading of ' disposition,' and its appearance there suggests what lessons might best be learned from the classics, and illustrates the peculiar relations between the new poets and the humanists. The study of ' disposition,' as has already been noted, means study of classical methods, and it was a valuable study, since it taught poets to regard a poem as a unity, to look at it as a whole, not as a series of episodes. Along with the idea of ' kind,' it helped to reform the looseness of mediaeval poetry, because it forced the poet to realize clearly for himself what he was at and where he was aiming.

In such a poem as *Mother Hubberds Tale* the mediaeval method could be followed to a successful conclusion,

because Spenser had excellent models of fable in the
Bible and in older English poetry and prose ; the tales
of Gower, and still more the short satirical poems of the
Middle Ages, the *fabliaux*, had in full measure the virtues
of conciseness and steady progress to a foreseen end,
for their simple concern was with that end and with the
single point they were trying to satirize or illustrate.
But the average mediaeval poet, when he engaged on
work on a large scale, became entangled in description
and detail, and failed to reconcile the interest of the
moment with the interest of the whole.   It is part of
Chaucer's greatness that he was aware of this danger,
but even he fell into it at times.   Now the new poets
meant to work on the large scale, and the lesson of form,
as a thing to be considered and consciously observed in
planning and execution, was very valuable, and especially
to Spenser, for *The Faerie Queene*, like any long poem,
was built up of passages of varying length in pursuance
of the poet's purposes, in accordance with the different
sources from which he drew his matter, and in conse-
quence of the accidents of composition : the analysis of
The Ruines of Time in the last chapter exemplifies the
working of these conditions on the smaller scale.   The
episodic conduct of the story, inherited through Ariosto
from the mediaeval romancers, tended still more to make
the organization of the poem difficult, and the measure
of value in *The Faerie Queene* is the dexterity with which
most of its transitions of thought are made, and the
extraordinary juxtaposition without mutual interference
of episodes so diverse in subject and content and so
equally brilliant in execution.

Form, then, and the constant sense of form, were
needed and were developed, and with them came the

idea of style—form being indeed only the first and broadest consideration involved in the study of treatment, which is the study of style, of the way of writing. The great and noble poetry which the new poets desired to write required a noble and flexible style, and the notion of style, the idea that effective and beautiful expression was essential and that it could be learned or created by care and labour, was the first lesson of all the humanists gave. For the humanists were preoccupied with the study and teaching of style, and the poets their pupils could not but have it pressed on them daily, as they strove in school and college to acquire a latinity with the majestic finality of Cicero's, the neatness and point of Horace's, the grace and suggestiveness of Virgil's. The humanists' difficulty with the modern tongues has already been noticed : their empirical method postulated an existing subject of analysis and imitation. They could teach Latin style, and they might say with Ascham, ' And this not only to serve in the *Latin* and *Greke* tong, but also in our own English language,' but the primary virtues of their own Latin were ' purity ' and ' correctness,' which meant ' sanctioned by the usage of Cicero or Virgil ' ; they saw the same criterion imposed on Italian by their chieftain Bembo, and they were slow to acknowledge—though they could not deny—that the former did not apply to a mixed language in process of formation, nor the latter to a literature in which there was nothing to judge by. These notions had their use, as a brake on extravagance and carelessness, but driving force was needed first.

Some driving force the humanists could apply, by their comment on Cicero and Virgil and the rest, and by their teaching of formal rhetoric. They made their pupils study the expression of the masters in detail, imitate their finest passages, and learn the practical reasons for the rhythms and figures they copied, until elegance, precision, and strength became habitual ideas in their minds. English humanists had to do all this in Latin, because, in Ascham's phrase, ' the providence of God hath left unto us in no other tong, save onelie in the *Greke* and *Latin* tong, the trew preceptes and perfite examples of eloquence.' It was a failure, perhaps, that they should deduce that eloquence was impossible in English, as Ascham does in the prefaces to his *Toxophilus*, but after all their business was with Greek and Latin, and the new poets, as the natural innovators and leaders of style, soon made French and English theirs. Before long Ramus, whom Gabriel Harvey admired and copied, was illustrating his *Rhetoric* with quotations from Ronsard, and in England the transition was made by Mulcaster, the follower of du Bellay. The rhetorical study was valuable in any language. In Italy, as we have seen, the most influential opinion was satisfied with the Tuscan style of Petrarch and Boccaccio, as a fixed style to which later writers should conform and by which they might be tested, and Minturno, Pigna, Dolce, and many others, followed Dante and Dante's disciple Trissino in analysing style along with the other characteristics of Tuscan poetry. It was this certainty, approaching the classic, that gave Italian much of its prestige in the eyes of France and England : the Tuscan poet was working to a standard while the French and English were experimenting. But in the light of the event it may be doubted whether the lack of models of perfection in their own tongues were not an advantage to the latter. They had no one school of style, but learned from the

classics, from the Italians, and from their own country-
men, and out of the mass they created a living style of
their own.

The most obvious weakness of English poetry between Chaucer and Spenser is weakness of style. Spenser could not but contrast the baldness and diffuseness
of his elder contemporaries with the wealth of Virgil
and the pith of Horace, the laborious difficulty of Wyatt
with the ease and grace of Chaucer. He could not but
see that any superiority that Surrey had over Wyatt was
largely that Surrey was able to mould his English to the
sonnet-form where Wyatt could only cramp his. Sack-
ville's *Induction* in the *Mirror for Magistrates* was indeed
successful, but its scope was very limited. The work
that Spenser proposed to himself was greater, deeper,
and more various than all of these together ; he had
great matters to treat and great forms to create, and to
succeed he had to learn to write well. Also, since the
English language was so much altered in syntax since
the time of Chaucer, the one English master ' who language had at will '—who could say the things he wanted
to say in the way in which he wanted to say them—he
had to make a style for himself, a new style to suit the
new aims. It was forced on him, not only that his
verse might be beautiful, but that it might be intelligible.
Clarity is the first of the rhetorical virtues, and in the
modern languages it is often difficult to distinguish
whether a problem is one of syntax or one of style. The
order of words, for instance, which in the inflected languages affects emphasis and rhythm, is still more important in English, because it also expresses their relation,
that is, the meaning of the sentence they make up. This
is perfected in English largely by a kind of artistic tact,

rather than by rules, and this tact is acquired by the study of style. The school of thought of which Spenser and Sidney were the leaders, again, regarded poetry as a means to persuade men to righteousness. From whom, then, would they learn, if not from the rhetoricians, whose profession it was to teach the art of persuasion? They designed their own works, not merely for amusement or as a social elegance, but to affect the minds and hearts of their readers, and in so far their poetry partook of the nature of oratory, and, requiring the same skill, they learned in the same school. Indeed as poetry is higher than oratory, they required it the more, and as the poet is less bound by convention and rule, so he must understand the more profoundly.

Formal rhetoric was no novelty to poets, but these new poets of the sixteenth century were better artists, and they had more models, and higher and more varied purposes to serve, than their predecessors of the fourteenth and fifteenth. From Quintilian and Cicero they learned a more reasonable and less dogmatic theory of rhetoric than Skelton or Molinet learned from their mediaeval textbooks, and their firmer idea of their own importance as being the elect, as being poets, and of the value of the vulgar tongues as languages, kept them from extravagant servility to their masters. Above all they learned that first lesson of clarity—the briefest comparison of Spenser with Lidgate and Skelton will show how well he expresses his meaning, and not because he is simple in word or thought, but in his most elaborate passages—and this lucidity they gained along with another rhetorical virtue, conciseness. Critics have enlarged at times on the looseness of Spenser's style, his repetitions, his occasional wheeling about a fixed point. We do not, indeed, find in Spenser the compact phrase of Shakespeare, but for good reason. Shakespeare had only ' the two hours traffic of the stage ' in which to express his world of meaning, and for each passage only the moment during which it was spoken. He was forced, therefore, to compress, and forced to make each thought tell swiftly and vividly. Spenser wrote to be read by studious readers, had all the space of an epic at his command, and so could linger and elaborate as he pleased. In fact, however, and especially in comparison with his predecessors, his style is unusually close in texture, as E.K. noted : ' Now, for the knitting of sentences, which they call the joynts and members therof, and for al the compasse of the speach, it is round without roughnesse and learned without hardnes, such indeede as may be perceived of the leaste understoode of the moste, but judged onely of the learned. For what in most English wryters useth to be loose, and as it were ungyrt, in this Authour is well grounded, finely framed, and strongly trussed up together.' E.K. notes this as significant of the learned character of *The Shepheardes Calender*, for it is not only the result of classical discretion, but achieved by careful attention to the force and aptness of phrases and by the use of such rhetorical figures as repetition, which binds phrases together, metaphor, which enriches most in the shortest space, and a dozen more, used consciously and with artistic intention.

The skilful employment of the colours of rhetoric gives closeness of texture to style, but their principal use is for variety, and in this respect also Spenser may be compared with the earlier poets, and still more with the two writers of elaborate prose in his own time, Lyly and

Sidney, who weary the reader by their constant recourse to two or three figures, while Spenser, though he has his favourites, uses a wide range. Hazlitt complained of the monotony of Spenser's style ; it is true that the soft sweetness which Hazlitt found cloying is the effect which Spenser compassed most easily, but it is by no means his only effect. The violent ' high style ' of *The Teares of the Muses* may not be admired, but few English poets of the time could do the like, and fewer before it. There is great variety within *The Shepheardes Calender*, and in *Muiopotmos* Spenser indulged the play instinct that is an element in all art. ' Spenser seems to delight in his art for his own skill's sake. In the *Muiopotmos*, see the security and ostentation with which he draws out and refines his description of a butterfly's back and wings. . . . It is all like the working of an exquisite loom which strongly and unweariedly yields fine webs, for exhibition, and defiance of all spinners.' [1] Spenser certainly ' rhymed for fun ' here, like Burns, or as Chaucer did in the rhetorical catherine-wheel with which he closed the Clerk's Tale. By this time he had his English at will, and enjoyed it ; he had advanced from *The Shepheardes Calender*, in which his rhetorical training is so obvious as at times to overcome his taste, and in which E.K. delights to point out ' a prety Epanorthosis . . . and withall a Paronomasia,' or ' a patheticall parenthesis, to encrease a carefull hyperbaton,' to *The Faerie Queene*, where the style is not only gorgeous in certain passages and magnificent in others, but is varied at will from page to page with figures which seem inevitable.

This variety of style was not fortuitous, but controlled by the principle of ' decorum,' which links style closely

[1] Emerson, *Journals*, Vol. VII, p. 229.

with kind, form, and subject. E.K. claimed this also for his author : ' No lesse, I thinke, deserveth his wittinesse in devising, his pithinesse in uttering, his complaints of love so lovely, his discourses of pleasure so pleasantly, his pastoral rudenesse, his morall wisenesse, his dewe observing of Decorum everye where, in personages, in seasons, in matter, in speach ; and generally, in al seamely simplycitie of handeling his matter, and framing his words.' This principle Spenser rarely forgot. It lies behind the plainness of *Mother Hubberds Tale*, the fanciful elaboration of *Muiopotmos*, the learned inflation of *The Teares of the Muses*, as well as behind the rudeness of *The Shepheardes Calender*—though there, as if in deprecation of the poet's temerity, the rudeness is emphasized in those eclogues which treat of ecclesiastical politics—and the simplicity of *Colin Clouts Come Home Again*. Above all it is to be seen in *The Faerie Queene*. Spenser was an imitator, but he imitated many masters ; he had learned, as part of the imitative method, that the choice of a model was the first duty, and that the choice depended on the subject and the kind of poem he intended to write. So when we find the style of *Mother Hubberds Tale* Chaucerian, or that of *Muiopotmos* Ovidian, we may take it as caused by Spenser's sense of decorum. In *The Faerie Queene*, as we compare a chivalric passage like some early in the Fourth Book with a religious one like the end of the First, or pass, in the sixth Canto of the Third Book, from the clear smoothness of the Hue and Cry after Cupid to the philosophical solidity of the Gardens of Adonis, we may trace the 'influence' of Malory or Chaucer, of the Book of Revelations, of Plato, of Moschus or Tasso, of Lucretius ; we trace rather Spenser's selection and variation of style in accordance with the same dominant principle of congruity.

The operation of the principle of decorum may be watched in Spenser's use of the colours of rhetoric—the oratorical questions and exclamations of *The Teares of the Muses*, the ' epic ' similes of *The Faerie Queene*, the homely proverbs of *The Shepheardes Calender*—and more easily in his choice of similes and metaphors—those of hunting and hawking to suit the knightly subject of *The Faerie Queene*, those of country pursuits and pastimes for the mouths of his shepherds, those of the arts to fit the person of each of the Muses. It was the true appreciation of this artistic principle, the understanding that figures are not valuable in themselves, but only in their time and place, and that their purpose is not mere decoration, but the elucidation and impression of the mood and subject, that gave the new poets greater success in the application of their rhetorical acquirements, just as it was the rhetorical practice that gave them greater control over language than their elders, and greater facility and copiousness than their modern descendants. They were drilled in good expression until it became a habit, and the habit of observing decorum was not the least useful part of the discipline.

Decorum controlled the arrangement of phrase, the use and the choice of images and figures ; above all, it controlled the first element in style, the choice of words. In discussing the propriety of words in a poem, two questions have been asked : first, ' Is this word proper to the place, subject, and purpose ? ' and second, ' Is this word a proper word to use at all ? ' The first question was obviously present in Spenser's mind throughout all his work. The variety of style in his poems is due to real skill, as noted above, in all the art of writing, not merely to choice of words or word-forms, as some of his eighteenth-century imitators seem to have thought. Still, the careful selection of vocabulary to suit person and subject is the first thing to be noticed. Not only do the rusticity of *The Shepheardes Calender* and the archaism of *Mother Hubberds Tale* differ from the neologism of *Muiopotmos*, but the diction of *The Faerie Queene* varies from passage to passage just as widely. Nor is it enough to state that in, say, the sixth Canto of the Fourth Book Spenser was influenced by Malory, whereas in the sixth Canto of the Third Book he was under classical influence : Spenser took the episode (of the disguised knights fighting in ignorance of each other's identity) from Malory, and he took also the words of Malory in order to give the passage an antique and chivalric flavour in accordance with its antique and chivalric subject and ethic. To have given the same atmosphere to the two classical myths in the other Canto would have destroyed their value, would have been wrong just as it would have been wrong to make the Muses speak like the shepherds.

In any particular instance ' decorum ' would be his defence against all cavillers. Sidney objected to ' that same framing of his stile to an old rustick language ' in *The Shepheardes Calender*,[1] but Buchanan's pupil King James knew the reason of it : ' Ye man lykewayis tak heid that ye waill your wordis according to the purpose. . . . Gif your purpose be of landwart effairis, to use corruptit and uplandis wordis.'[2] By a little special pleading Spenser might defend even his anomalies. The

---

[1] *Apologie, Eliz. Crit. Essays*, I, 196.
[2] *Ane Schort Treatise, ibid.*, 217–8.

dialects of his shepherds are mixed, and the *Calender* contains foreign and learned words which no real shepherd would know : but Spenser was not trying to write realistic poems either about or for shepherds ; these were pastorals, examples of a scholarly artificial form which Virgil had used, and half the point of the business is just that these shepherds were not real shepherds, but poets and scholars and bishops, and even a queen was among them, so that learned words, though unsuitable to the supposed persons, were quite in keeping with the real, as they were with the subjects of the poems, with the kind, and with the audience to whom they were addressed. This argument would then be met by an appeal to the second question, the general question of propriety. But this demands separate study, for it is significantly characteristic of the views of the new poets and it was important to the future of English poetry.

The difficulty the humanists had in applying their critical standards to the modern tongues is particularly obvious in this question of diction. English scholars of the Cambridge group had to compromise in their ideas of purity and correctness, for it was obvious that English was not a pure language and that it required reinforcement; nor did a standard of correct usage exist. Thus their teaching came to be almost entirely negative. After all they never did believe in the vernacular ; a simple speech and a homely style sufficed for the simple ideas they would treat of in English, and so, naturally enough, they went no further. A new conception of language was necessary, a new approach to the problem, and this, as has been observed, was suggested by Speroni, extended by Minturno, reduced to practice—

perhaps with the help of Dante—by du Bellay and Ronsard, and passed on to Spenser by Mulcaster. Speroni made it clear that language was not static, but capable of increase and improvement ; his academic theory, however, made him stop there and accept the humanistic method of Bembo.

Minturno drew the distinction between the dead languages and the living : '*Ferrante Carafa* : I give you infinite thanks, Signor Minturno, that you have this day freed me from that superstition in which some bind themselves tight who are held as masters and censors of the Tuscan tongue. *M*. What superstition is that ? *F*. That in prose no word . . . should be employed which is not used by Boccaccio, and in poetry no word not spoken by Petrarch. *M*. If this strictness of diction ought to obtain, it should certainly be in the Latin tongue, as in one that has been abandoned for many and many a year. . . . Sannazaro, brightest light of Latin epic poetry, shows and concludes that so strict a law need not be observed in that. Now, how much the less ought it to be observed in our own, which we take in with our mothers' milk and use, as proper, natural, and maternal, in the manifestation of our thoughts. . . . For in every age whatever tongue you please underwent some alteration in words. . . . And with reason, since speech does not proceed from nature, which makes things similar in all places and at all times, but from the will of man, which is in itself mutable. . . . Speech is like money, which changes its use and its form in different regions and at different times. Hence, as Horace teaches, it has always been permissible, and always will be, to find words, so long as they are of that stamp as is in use in our own age. . . . And why should that be

forbidden to us that Dante, Cino, Cavalcante and Petrarch permitted to themselves ?   For each of them used
words which they did not read in the works of their
predecessors.   But since this is an old problem and
full of controversy and often discussed in the discourses
of the most learned men, from their opinion and yours
and mine let us decide that simple words be taken from
the most excellent writers of those times which gained
greatest praise for writing good and correct Tuscan ;
if they are not found in them, then from the others who
flourished after them.   If still less in these, let recourse
be had to the foreign, and more to the Latins than to the
others, as we find the ancients have taught. . . .   But
where something meets us so new that no word, either
Tuscan or foreign, is found to speak of it, it will be right
to form a new word to signify it.'[1]   This is a more
logical conclusion than Speroni drew from his premises,
but still it is calculated for a developed language.   The
French were forced by their more necessitous language
to experiment, to discuss, and to be daring and positive.
Before Minturno's treatise was published, du Bellay
had asserted the freedom of the poet, and though Ronsard borrowed arguments from the Italian, he had already
taken up a more advanced position.

It is a commonplace of criticism that Spenser, in Ben
Jonson's phrase, ' writ no language.'   His is an artificial
speech constructed for his own purposes out of many
and various elements, and that with the intention of
supplying and beautifying the English language, as we
may judge from E.K.'s condemnation of objectors :

---

[1] *L'Arte Poetica*, 446.   Sidney was ' much advantaged ' by Minturno
in his *Apologie* (see Mr. Gregory Smith's notes), and thus, if in no other
way, Spenser may have been introduced to the Italian.

' The last, more shameful then both, that of their owne country and natural speach, which together with their Nources milk they sucked, they have so base regard and bastard judgement, that they will not onely themselves not labor to garnish and beautifie it, but also repine, that of other it should be embellished. Like to the dogge in the maunger, that him selfe can eate no hay, and yet barketh at the hungry bullock, that so faine would feede : whose currish kind, though it cannot be kept from barking, yet conne I them thank that they refrain from byting.' When this artificial speech is analysed, it is seen to be constructed on just the lines advocated by du Bellay and Ronsard, and to be in contradiction of contemporary English opinion except—so far as we know it—that of Mulcaster, so that E.K.'s anticipation of censure was not unfounded.

E.K. confines himself almost entirely to his Author's revival of old words from Chaucer, Langland, and Malory : ' And first of the wordes to speake, I graunt they be something hard, and of most men unused, yet both English, and also used of most excellent authors and most famous Poetes.' ' If any will rashly blame such his purpose in choyse of old and unwonted words, him may I more justly blame and condemn . . . for in my opinion it is one special prayse of many, which are dew to this Poete, that he hath laboured to restore, as to theyr rightful heritage, such good and naturall English words, as have ben long time out of use, and almost clean disinherited. Which is the only cause, that our Mother tonge, which truely for it selfe is both ful enough for prose, and stately enough for verse, hath long time ben counted most bare and barrein of both.' This seems close enough to Minturno's position, but the change of

language between Chaucer and Spenser, compared with
that between Petrarch and Minturno, was so great as
to make Chaucer's English strange. E.K. is aware that
this statement is heresy, and hints broadly at two authorities which might be brought against him. ' For albe,
amongst many other faultes, it be specially objected of
Valla against Livie, and of other against Sallust, that
with over much studie they affect antiquitye . . . yet I
am of opinion, and eke the best learned are of the lyke,
that these ancient solemn words are a great ornament.'
That ' other ' was Sir John Cheke, as appears from Ascham's *Scholemaster*,[1] and though Ascham himself was
inclined to an old fashion of speech, and though he explains that Cheke's objection to Sallust's archaisms was
mainly that they did not appear in Cicero, yet he quotes
the objection with some emphasis, and it is clear that
E.K., and so probably Spenser himself, read the remark
as an objection to archaism in general.

Again, E.K. complains that ' Other some, not so wel
seene in the English tonge as perhaps in other languages,
if they happen to here an olde word, albeit very naturall
and significant, crye out streightway, that we speak no
English, but gibbrish, or rather such as in old time
Evanders mother spake.' Which is perhaps a reminiscence of Wilson, the only humanist of the Cambridge
group to give formal instruction for writers in English,
who borrowed from Aulus Gellius, in his *Arte of Rhetor-
ique* (which was probably among Spenser's textbooks),
the story of how ' Phavorinus the Philosopher . . . did
hit a yong man over the Thumbes very handsomely,
for using of over old, and over straunge wordes. Sirha
(quoth he) when our olde great auncesters and Graund-

---

[1] *Elizabethan Critical Essays*, I, 39–44.

sires were alive, they spake plainly in their mothers
tongue, and used olde language, such as was spoken then
at the building of Roome. But you talke me such a
Latine, as though you spake with them even now, that
were two or three thousand yeres agoe.'[1] It is with
scorn that Wilson notes that ' the fine courtier will speake
nothing but *Chaucer*,'[2] a remark which suggests that
Spenser might have been influenced by a court fashion.
Certainly Spenser could have pointed to the *Mirror for
Magistrates* and the courtly *Songes and Sonettes* published
by Tottel, but these belonged to an earlier generation,
and the first objection to Spenser's diction came from the
leader of court poetry in Spenser's own day, from his
patron Sidney himself, to whom *The Shepheardes Calender*
was dedicated.

Thus the two young Cambridge men departed from
the Cambridge doctrine—and the doctrine of the school
of Cheke was probably even stronger in the oral tradition
of the University than in the written treatises—and dis-
agreed with the fashion of the men to whom Spenser was
looking for advancement. E.K.'s argument was new in
English, as was the deliberate intention of the author he
was justifying, but it was familiar by this time in France,
where the Pléiade set out with the same deliberate intention of enriching and embellishing contemporary speech,
and found their first resource in the old French poetry.
Thus du Bellay advises his reader : ' Use purely French
words, not too commonplace and not too unusual, unless
sometimes you care to take over, and as it were inset like
a precious and rare stone, some ancient words in your
poem, after the manner of Virgil, who used this word
olli for *illi*, *aulai* for *aulae*, and so on. To do this, you

[1] Ed. G. H. Mair, p. 3.   [2] P. 162.

must see all those old French romances and poets, where
you will find *ajourner* for *faire jour* . . . and a thousand
other fine words which we have lost by our negligence.
Doubt not but the moderate usage of such words gives
great majesty to verse as to prose, as do the relics of
saints to the crosses and other sacred jewels dedicated to
the temples.'[1] On the same lines he justifies his own
usage in his translation of Virgil : ' I have used *gallees*
for *galleres* . . . *isnel* for *leger* . . . and others whose
antiquity (following the example of my author Virgil)
seems to me to give a certain majesty to the verse.'[2]
The same precept and the same practice are to be found
in the work of Ronsard. ' You will not reject the old
words of our romances, but will select them with mature
and prudent choice.'[3] ' You will not disdain old French
words, inasmuch as I consider them always vigorous,
whatever may be said, until they have borne to fill their
place, like an old stock, a sprout.'[4] To an example in
La Franciade he attached the characteristic marginal
note : ' Our critics will laugh at this old French word ;
but they must just be allowed to babble. On the con-
trary, I am of opinion that we should retain significant
old words until usage has forged other new ones in their
place.'[5] Archaism is not predominant in Ronsard's
style as it is in Spenser's ; he observed the discretion he
continually recommended. His motive was almost
entirely linguistic, for only occasionally, as in *La Franciade*, was he moved by considerations of decorum to
suggest remoteness and age. Yet that reinforces, rather

---

[1] *Deff. et Ill.*, p. 129.   [2] *Epistre* before the translation.
[3] *Art Poétique*, p. 321.   [4] *Ibid.*, p. 335.
[5] Ed. Blanchemain, Vol. III, p. 150.

than supersedes, the principle. The French poets did not teach Spenser to love Chaucer, but they taught him to be bold in regarding him as the 'well of English undefiled' and in drawing upon his store of language. The use of dialect is closely allied to the habit of archaism, as E.K. observed : 'such olde and obsolete words are most used of country folk.' Sidney described the speech of *The Shepheardes Calender* as 'an old rustick language,' and disapproved of it. Puttenham, a later representative of the Cambridge purists, condemned dialect in spite of its comparative purity : 'Neither shall he take the terms of the Nothernmen, such as they use in dayly talke . . . nor in effect any speech used beyond the river of Trent, though no man can deny that theirs is the purer English Saxon at this day, yet it is not so Courtly nor so currant as our Southerne English is ; no more is the far Westerne mans speach.'[1] The basis of Spenser's language is certainly a courtly Southern English, but decorum prescribed rusticity in the eclogues, and he had good authority for the use of dialect words and forms in Ronsard, who probably knew Speroni's *Dialogo delle Lingue* as did du Bellay, but came to the opposite conclusion. 'You will not reject the old Picardy verbs, like *voudroye* for *voudroy, aimeroye, diroye, feroye.*'[2] Ronsard belonged to the Vendomois, and loved his native dialect, but it is that of Picardy he recommends here, because it is the most ancient ; he returns to the point in the second preface to *La Franciade*. Spenser was a Londoner born and bred, and it would require more than a vague sentiment of northern ancestry and a doubtful holiday visit to 'the North country' to

---

[1] *Elizabethan Critical Essays*, II, p. 150.
[2] *Art Poétique*, p. 333.

produce the strange dialect of his work, and still more the courage to publish it. In any case, his words and forms are not all northern ; though northern forms predominate, it is probably for their antiquity, and the value of dialect is pressed by Ronsard for other reasons. ' You will dexterously choose and appropriate to your work the most significant words of the dialects of our France, when you have not such good or proper ones in your own nation ; and one need not trouble whether the words are Gascon, Poitevin, Norman, Manceaux, Lyonnais, or of other districts, provided they are good and that they signify precisely what you wish to say.' [1] Here, then, as in the question of archaism, Spenser agreed with the French poets as against the English critics. There is far more of dialect in *The Shepheardes Calender* than in any work of the Pléiade, for which the plea of decorum might be adduced, but even more that of inexperience ; dialect in *The Faerie Queene* is largely for the suggestion of antiquity ; but it appears in almost all Spenser's poems, and the linguistic purpose is indubitable.

A third source of vocabulary exploited by the Pléiade was the great mass of language in daily use in the arts, professions, and trades, the technical terms whose employment might add force and precision both to description and to figure. ' Again I wish to advise you to frequent sometimes not only the learned, but also all sorts of workmen and mechanics, such as sailors, foundrymen, painters, engravers, and others, to know their inventions, the names of the materials, of the tools, and the terms used in their arts and industries, in order to draw thence those fine comparisons and lively descrip-

[1] P. 321 ; see also the second Preface to *La Franciade*, pp. 32 and 34.

tions of all things.'[1] ' You will frequent often workmen
of all trades, as of shipping, venery, falconry, and principally those who work with fire, goldsmiths, founders,
smiths, metal-workers ; and thence you will draw many
fine and lively comparisons with the technical terms of
the trades, to enrich your work and make it more agreeable and perfect.'[2] It is improbable that this would
have commended itself to Wilson, who complained of
the crabbed speech of lawyers, auditors, and of ' dark
language ' generally, and Puttenham certainly disapproved : ' We finde in our English writers many
wordes and speaches amendable . . . and many dark
wordes and not usuall nor well sounding, though they
be dayly spoken in Court.'[3] Spenser, however, understood as well as Ronsard the importance of the fine and
lively comparison, and the value of the precise term.
The Faerie Queene is full of the terms of hunting and
hawking, and Spenser displays some acquaintance with
terms of seamanship, of art, of archery, of armoury, and,
naturally in view of his employment, of law. These
are used as a rule in figures of speech or as proper to
the episode in which they appear, but the usage is not
always entirely figurative, and the fact of their use at
all is notable.[4]

[1] Du Bellay, *Deff. et Ill.*, p. 147.

[2] Ronsard, *Art Poétique*, p. 321.

[3] *Elizabethan Critical Essays*, II, 151.

[4] A very few examples of Spenser's technicalities may serve : *hawking*,
F.Q. V, iv, 42 ; *sea*, F.Q. I, xi, 10, I, xii, 1 ; *architecture*, F.Q. IV, x, 6 ;
law of chivalry, F.Q. V, iii, 37 ; *law*, F.Q. VI, vii, 36. Mr. Whitman's
Subject Index will assist the curious.

The history of the problem of technicalities in poetry is interesting :
Milton's avoidance of them is notorious—he follows Minturno, ' where
a new thing confronts you, and there is no Tuscan or foreign word to
describe it, you may make a new one, *or, it will be safer, describe it with*

Before the native speech could be considered as exhausted, another expedient remained : the construction of new forms from existing words, ancient and modern. This the Pléiade called by the horticultural term of *provignement*—layering—and it is best described in their own words : ' All words, whatever they are, in use or out of use, if there remain any part of them, whether in noun, verb, adverb, or participle, you can by good and certain analogy make to increase and multiply, since our tongue is still poor, and one must take trouble, although people may murmur, with all discretion to enrich and cultivate it. Example of old words : since the noun *verve* remains to us, you can make from the noun the verb *verver* and the adverb *vervement* ; from the noun *essoine, essoiner, essoinement,* and a thousand such others. And when there is only the adverb, you can freely and boldly make the verb and the participle. At the worst you will note it in the margin of your book, to make its meaning understood. And from words received in use like *pays, eau, feu,* you will make *payser, ever, fover, evement, fovement,* and a thousand other such words which do not yet see the light for want of a bold and fortunate adventurer.'[1] This form of innovation is one of the distinguishing marks of Spenser's style : the reader need not look far for ' dreriment,' ' embrave,' ' joyance,' and ' a thousand such others.' The compound epithet is in the same category, a device which commended itself to Sidney : ' [The English language]

---

many words.' The change of opinion may be observed in Dryden, between *Annus Mirabilis,* which is full of technicalities, and his latest works, in which he avoids them. The relation with the trend of French criticism is clear enough.

[1] Ronsard, *Art Poétique,* p. 335.

is particularly happy in compositions of two or three words together, neere the Greeke, far beyond the Latine : which is one of the greatest beauties can be in a language.'[1] It is unnecessary to ascribe Spenser's adoption of the compound epithet to the influence of Sidney, for Spenser knew the sources from which Sidney took it— Ronsard, du Bellay, du Bartas, Henri Estienne. Sidney's term ' composition ' echoes the French ' mots composez comme *pie-sonnant, porte-lois, porte-ciel.*'[2] Though the origin is Greek, the immediate source was French, and it is the comparative frequency of compound epithets in *Muiopotmos* that, more than any other one characteristic, betrays Spenser's debt to France for the elegance of that poem.

This cultivation of the native tongue, however, was insufficient for the requirements of the new poetry, and the new poets had recourse to foreign tongues, ancient and modern, for the further increase of vocabulary. This was the most bitterly contested ground of all. Sir John Cheke might have been claimed by Spenser as a precedent for his experiments in ' provignement,' but not for borrowing. ' I am of this opinion that our own tung shold be written cleane and pure, unmixt and unmangled with borowing of other tungs. . . . For then doth our tung naturallie and praisablie utter her meaning, when she boureweth no counterfeitness of other tunges to attire herself withall, but useth plainlie her own with such shift, as nature, craft, experiens, and

---

[1] *Elizabethan Critical Essays*, I, 204.

[2] Du Bellay, *Epistre* before the translation of Virgil. Minturno touches on the compound epithet, *L'Arte Poetica*, 448, but considers it suitable only in comedy. See Sir Sidney Lee's *French Renaissance in England*, p. 245 ff.

folowing of other excellent doth lead her unto, and if
she want at ani tijm (as being unperfight she must) yet
let her borow with suche bashfulnes, that it mai appeer,
that if either the mould of our own tung could serve us
to fascion a woord of our own, or if the old denisoned
wordes could content and ease this neede, we wold not
boldly venture of unknowen wordes.' [1] Ascham, Wilson,
Puttenham take the same line, and in this question
E.K., perhaps to strengthen the case for archaism and
dialect, is faithful to his Cambridge masters : ' Which
default whenas some endevoured to salve and recure,
they patched up the holes· with peces and rags of other
languages, borrowing here of the French, there of the
Italian, every where of the Latine ; not weighing how
il those tongues accorde with themselves, but much
worse with ours : So now they have made our English
tongue a gallimaufray, or hodgepodge of al other speches.'
On the other side were Sir Thomas Elyot, who desired
to enrich English with high rhetorical and philosophical
terms, the translators who experienced daily the difficulty of rendering from highly developed languages
into one less developed, and a less vocal but probably
numerous company who took up the common-sense
position that borrowing was inevitable. Du Bellay
was quite clear on the subject : ' I would advise anyone
who undertakes a great work that he fear not to invent,
adopt, and compose in imitation of the Greeks some
French words.' [2] ' It is not a vice, but very laudable, to
borrow from a foreign tongue sentences and words,
and appropriate them to one's own.' [3] Ronsard coun-
selled discretion, but his own practice was sufficiently

---

[1] Letter to Hoby; in Arber's introduction to *Scholemaster*.
[2] *Deff. et Ill.*, p. 125.   [3] P. 72.

7

bold, and Mulcaster had no doubts whatever. ' When the mind is fraught with matter to deliver, it is still in pain untill it have delivered, and therefore to have the deliverie such, as maie discharge the thing well, and content all parties it seketh both home helps, where theie be sufficient, and significant, and where the own home yeildeth nothing at all, or not pithie enough, it craveth help of that tung, from whence it received the matter of deliverie.' Spenser's borrowing received little attention in his own time, which is the best proof of his discretion, but he used his privilege to borrow from Greek and Latin, Italian and French, at will, and brought into currency some borrowings as well as some revivals.

For all this, of course, the new poets could adduce authority : Cicero, Quintilian, and above all Horace, had given licence to the poet to revive and innovate.[1] The point to be observed is that—in spite of Minturno's exception of Sannazaro—the humanists did not view the matter in the same light. Du Bellay might quote the precedent of Virgil for his archaisms, but the humanist took Virgil as a model, not as a precedent : there is a world of difference. Nor is an authority the same thing as an inspiration. It was the early reading of ' Jean Lemaire de Belges, the Romance of the Rose, and the works of Clément Marot,' not the study of the *Ars Poetica*, that bred the love of quaint and pithy old phrases and the taste that employed them for the enrichment of new verse. Ronsard and du Bellay did not turn from Cinthio or Pigna to search ' Lancelot and Gawain ' for the material of epic ; they found there the justification of their natural pleasure, and were no doubt the bolder

[1] Cicero : *Orator*, XX, 68 ; *de Oratore*, II, xiv, 60, III, 38, and cf. E.K. ; Quintilian : X, xxviii ff. ; Horace, *Ars Poetica*, 45-72.

for the authority. So also Spenser loved his Chaucer,
and, in E.K.'s excellent phrase, 'having the sound of
those auncient Poetes still ringing in his eares, he mought
needes in singing hit out some of theyr tunes.' But
the tunes were none the worse for E.K.'s quotation of
Cicero to justify them.

The Pléiade ruled out of court much of the humanist
criticism, and proclaimed the higher status of the poet.
' The poets, being the boldest, have been the first to
forge and compose words, which for their beauty and
expressiveness have passed by the mouth of the orators
and the common people, then finally have been received,
praised, and admired by everyone.'[1] Since, then, the
poet is the leader in the noble work of cultivating the
mother tongue, he must be free to experiment, without
restriction by pedantry or conservatism : ' To wish to
take away from a learned man who desires to enrich his
language the freedom to adopt unfamiliar words sometimes, would be to bind our language—which is not yet
rich enough—under a more rigorous law than the Greeks
and Romans gave themselves.'[2] The ear of the trained
and competent poet is the last court of appeal, and ' the
more words we have in our language the more perfect it
will be.'[3] ' And you will not care what the vulgar say
about you.'[4] Ronsard's word *vulgaire* might best be
translated ' stupid people,' for it includes all, princes or
pedants, who were not interested in the Pléiade enthusiasm for progress in poetry, but looked for sweet and
simple rhyming and for nothing more.

The new poets insisted on the serious importance of

---

[1] Ronsard, *Art Poétique*, p. 335.
[2] Du Bellay, *Deff. et Ill.*, p. 127.
[3] *Art Poétique*, p. 333. [4] *Ibid.*, p. 335.

their vernacular and the works they wrote in it, and
Spenser had the good fortune to be brought up in this
idea. The general objection of the purists against
unusual words was that such words were difficult, but
Mulcaster was not, like Ascham, writing in simple
fashion for the benefit of the unlettered, but a scholar
treating in a well-studied style a matter which demanded
serious consideration, and he expected something more
than casual or condescending attention, some of the
pains commonly bestowed only on the classics. ' For
mine own words, and the terms, that I use, theie be
generallie *English*. And if anie be either an incorporate
stranger, or otherwise translated [*i.e.* used figuratively
or in an unusual sense], or quite coined a new, I have
shaped it as fit for the place, where I use it, as my cunning will give me. And to be bold that waie for either
enfranchising the foren, or translating our own, without
to manifest insolence, or to wanton affection, or else to
invent new upon evident note, which will bear witness,
that it fitteth well, where it is to be used . . . till oft
using do make it well known, we are sufficiently war-
ranted both by president and precept of them, that can
judge best.'[1] ' In the force of words . . . there are to
be considered *commonesse* for every man, *beawtie* for the
learned, *braverie* to ravish, *borowing* to enlarge our natural
speche, and readiest deliverie. . . . And therefor if
anie reader find falt with anie word, which is not sutable
to his ear, bycause it is not he, for whom that word serves,
let him mark his own, which he knoweth, and make
much of the other, which is worthie his knowing. Know
you not som words ? Why ? no marvell. It is a metaphor, a learned translation, removed from where it is

[1] *Elementarie,* p. 268.

proper, into som such place where it is more properly
used, and most significant to, if it be well understood :
take pains to know it, you have of whom to learn. . . .
Is it a stranger ? but no Turk. And tho it were an
enemies word, yet good is worth the getting, tho it be
from your fo, as well by speche of writers, as by spoill of
soldiers. . . . He that hath skill in language, whether
learned and old, or liked and new, will not wonder at
words which he knoweth whence theie ar, neither marvell at a conceit quickly delivered, the like whereof he
meteth oft abrode.'[1] ' He must take acquaintance and
make the thing familiar if it seme to be strange. For
all strange things seme great novelties, and hard of enter-
tainment at their first arrivall, till theie be acquainted :
but after acquaintance they be verie familiar, and easie
to entreat. And words likewise, which either conveie
strange matters, or be strangers themselves, either in
name or in use, be no wilde beasts, tho theie be unwont,
neither is a term a *Tiger* to prove untractable. Familiar-
itie and acquaintance will cause facilitie, both in matter
and in words.'[2]

Had we *The English Poet*, the critical treatise which
Spenser wrote before he published *The Shepheardes
Calender*, we should probably find, under the heading
of Elocution, a theory of linguistic development equivalent to that of the Pléiade, and a reflection of the boldness of Mulcaster, acclaiming ' the conquering mind,
such as he must have, which either sekes himself, or is
desirous to se his cuntrie tung enlarged, and the same
made the instrument of all his knowledge, as it is of his
needs,' bold in claiming liberty to use ' the latest terms '
' either of pure necessitie in new matters, or of mere

[1] *Elementarie*, pp. 268–9.   [2] *Ibid.*, p. 263.

braverie, to garnish itself withal.'   For the same method
is constant in Spenser's work.   The principle of decorum
prescribes the preponderance of certain elements in *The
Shepheardes Calender* and *The Faerie Queene*, but the same
mingling of archaism, dialect, technical terms, and
learned and foreign words may be seen in the minor
poems also, and often where it would be difficult to allege
the sanction of decorum.   The terms of philosophy are
indispensable in the Platonic *Fowre Hymnes*, but they
appear also in the sonnets ;   the general character of the
diction of *The Teares of the Muses* is learned and latinized,
as the subject requires, but it is full also of archaisms like
aread, stowre, ycrept ;   the technical *catastrophees* and
diapase are suitable to their speakers, but a hunting
phrase, ' *rime at riot*,' is not.   Mother Hubberd's speech
is old-fashioned and familiar, but she indulges in legal
terms of the Irish courts, *cyted*, and *tort*, and *flaunt*, and
in classicisms like *diademe* and *lucid*, and so also, though
it is not surprising to find *humid* and *caerule* in a version
of Virgil, *whelky, batt, stound, rulesse, gride*, scarcely
sort with them.   Nor was Spenser entirely consistent
in the meanings of words :   he has several meanings
for *aread*, three for the Chaucerian *chevissance* (of which
one, its use as a flower-name in the April Eclogue, is
unexplained), three at least for *stound*.   His phrases are
precise, but his language frequently impressionistic.

This assertion of the freedom of the poet in dealing
with language would justify another characteristic of
the new poetry, the alteration of words for convenience
of rhyme and metre.   Puttenham devoted a whole chapter to the destruction of this heresy : ' Now there cannot
be in a maker a fowler fault then to falsifie his accent to
serve his cadence, or by untrue orthographie to wrench

his words to helpe his rime.'[1]   Gascoigne permitted it, though with more than a suspicion of satire in his phrase : ' This poeticall license is a shrewd fellow, and covereth many faults in a verse ; it maketh wordes longer, shorter, of mo sillables, of fewer, newer, older, truer, falser ; and to conclude, it turkeneth all things at pleasure,'[2] and in allowing this licence, though not in his satire, Gascoigne was following his original, Ronsard. ' When you find words which are difficult to rhyme, like *or*, *char*, and a thousand others, rhyme them boldly with *fort*, *ort*, *accort* . . . removing by license the last letter.'[3]   ' You will say, according as your verse constrains you, *or*, *ore*, *ores* . . . and a thousand others which you will shorten and lengthen without fear as it may please you.'[4]   Ronsard had indeed claimed the privilege in the preface to his first book, the *Odes* of 1550 : ' You will not find annoying if I have sometimes changed the letter E into A, and A often into E, taking away a letter from a word, or adding it, to make my rhyme more sonorous and perfect : truly such license had always been allowed in lengthy works.' Du Bellay expressed himself less boldly in the *Epistre* before his translation of the Fourth Book of the *Æneid*, but he was none the less bold in practice.

And boldest of all was Spenser, masterful at times, perhaps, rather than masterly, but bold in facing a situation which called for boldness. For the purposes of great poetry English was practically a new language ;

---

[1] *Elizabethan Critical Essays*, II, 84.

[2] *Ibid.*, I, 54, see Gabriel Harvey's annotations to Gascoigne's work among Mr. Gregory Smith's notes.

[3] *Art Poétique*, p. 328 : the whole passage is in the same vein.

[4] *Ibid.*, p. 333.

it had to be made, and Spenser, taught by Mulcaster and by those French poets from whom Mulcaster had learned, saw that it must be made by a poet and not by grammarians and set himself to be that poet. He treated the English language as if it belonged to him and not he to it. It was the grammarians' business to deduce the principles of language from his usage, not his to restrain his artistic sense of language by their rules. By his assumption of the primacy of the artist in this question of language Spenser merely bore out the underlying principle of all classicist criticism ; by carrying it over into English poetry he proved himself the more clearly to belong to the European movement.

CHAPTER IV

Verse and Metre

Spenser had to remake the English language for his own high purposes, and he developed a style peculiarly Spenserian—a style which is easily recognized as his and no one else's. He had also to make his own discoveries in versification and find his own solutions to its problems. The two processes are really one. The poet's indulgence in or avoidance of inversion, his habitual speed, his lofty vein or downright simplicity, the pointedness or the periodic rotundity of his phrase, his sense of tone and his taste in language—all these affect his choice of metres and his treatment of them ; and conversely, his temperamental feeling for rhythm, his power of sustaining it, his capacity for blending and varying it, are all factors governing his choice of words and disposition of phrases. In good poetry meaning, style and verse all work together to produce the unified expression, the effect, for which the poet is striving. It is the unity of effect that is notable, and noticeably new, in Spenser's work, a unity all the more remarkable that diction, style, and verse were, at once and together, the object of experiment and invention.

The novelty and the interest of *The Shepheardes Calender* lies in the variety of metre and the skill with which verse is handled, no less than in the interest and the importance of form and matter. This variety of metre was without precedent among Spenser's bucolic models, but it may be that, well aware of the monotony of certain mediaeval collections, he determined to add this variety also to the variety of subject and style. We cannot tell how many metres he had experimented with before, but there are thirteen in *The Shepheardes Calender*, and the couplet quoted by E.K. in his gloss to *October*, line 90, adds another to the list.[1] Of these three or four were common in his time ; two at least were entirely new inventions, three were new rhyme-arrangements, two new importations, one an imitation of Chaucerian couplet peculiar to this book : and only three of the thirteen were ever used by Spenser again. His freedom and resource are demonstrated again in the original rhyme-scheme of the *Amoretti* and the dedicatory sonnets prefixed to *The Faerie Queene*—though he had used a commoner arrangement in the *Visions*—in the invention of the curious metre of the fourth Epigram and still more of *The Faerie Queene* stanza, and in the brilliant adaptation of the Italian *canzone* in *Epithalamion* and *Prothalamion*.[2]

Some of these metres he derived from foreign sources —the canzone, as has been said, the *August* sestina, and, obviously, the sonnet, from Petrarch, though indeed the sonnet was by this time a European and not merely an Italian possession. If we are to take E.K.'s term literally, where he quotes the couplet

> The silver swanne doth sing before her dying day
> As shee that feeles the deepe delight that is in death

as from ' one of his sonetts,' then Spenser's sonnetteering

---

[1] See Appendix, A, p. 189.
[2] See Appendix, B and C, pp. 189–191.

began early, and the use of the alexandrine in sonnets
suggests the imitation of Ronsard : the word ' sonnet,'
however, was used so loosely in the sixteenth century
that we cannot be certain. The lyric stanzas of the
April and *December* songs are obviously learned in the
school of the Pléiade, but if he sought advice from Ronsard's critical works he would be encouraged—if encour-
agement were needed—to turn to Chaucer, for Ronsard
sends his reader for examples and models back to the
old French poets. From Chaucer came the couplet
and the habit of the rhymed stanza, and in using these
Spenser was but continuing an old English tradition.
But though a foreign verse-pattern might be copied, it
had to be adapted to the English language, and the direct
imitation of Chaucer was not entirely suitable to the
modern tongue. Spenser experimented unceasingly
with the rhymed stanza, even after he had found the
brilliant variation of *The Faerie Queene.* Beside the
common rhyme-scheme of the six-line stanza, which
makes it a quatrain and couplet on three rhymes, he made
one on two rhymes in *October* ; in *Daphnaida* he rearranged the rhymes of Rhyme Royal, and in *June* made
an eight-line stanza on two rhymes.[1] Of the couplet,
again, he tried three varieties, for before he settled down
to the regular ten-syllable ' heroic ' of *Mother Hubberds
Tale* he had written twelve-syllable couplets in the
Epilogue to *The Shepheardes Calender*, and in *February*,
May, and *September* had tried a curious experiment in
imitation of Chaucer's couplet as it would be read by his
contemporaries. Spenser must have had some notion
of the secret of the accented final *e* and *es* in Chaucerian
verse, for some of his own lines, even in *The Faerie Queene*,

[1] See Appendix, B, p. 189.

can hardly be scanned without this licence, but the verse
of these three eclogues can be understood at all only as
an attempt to reproduce the effect of Chaucer's verse
read without the final e's,[1] for though the majority of
the lines are of nine syllables, there may be as few as
eight and as many as eleven. The main metrical result
of the study of Chaucer, however, was the continuance
of the stanza and the determining of the ten-syllable line
as central to English metre.

The individuality of a poet, however, is shown less in
his choice of patterns than in his treatment of them.
Every writer has (if a mechanical metaphor be permitted) his own ' period of vibration,' the rhythm into
which he instinctively falls and by which any metre he
may choose to adopt is inevitably affected. Beside this
personal factor, there is the factor of style, and again
the factor of decorum, the ' suiting of sound to sense,'
defined once and for all in the *Essay on Criticism* by Pope,
who tried to abolish the personal factor and to confine the
poet to this alone. In all Spenser's verse we can hear
the long slow rhythm which was habitual to him. Only
once, in *March*, did he use the common romance metre,
and only once, in *July*, the common metre of six and eight,
and in both eclogues it is clear that he was fighting against
the lamentable tendency of these verse-forms to settle into
a jingling jog-trot. That tendency was one reason for
their popularity at the time ; it was easy for an incom-
petent poet to keep measure ; but Spenser had too fine
an ear, too strong a sense of rhythm, was too well trained
in critical principle and too ambitious, to endure unre-
lieved singsong. He knew that the principle of beauty

[1] With some hint, perhaps, from the loose four-beat line of *Piers
Plowman*.

in verse is the reconciliation of liberty and control—the
sense given to the reader (and still more to the speaker)
of a consistent pattern, the ' metre,' diversified by variations of rhythm which are never so violent as to obscure
or destroy that pattern, so that good verse is like a river,
which flows all in one direction, but carries on its surface
the changing play of eddies and ripples. Historically
considered, English verse is a compromise between the
strict French system and the free old English system ;
Chaucer and Gower had achieved this compromise, but
their work had to be done over again for modern English, and until Spenser no poet had appeared who was
great enough to do it.

The condition of English verse in Spenser's youth
is best described in Gascoigne's *Certayne Notes of Instruction*. ' Remember to holde the same measure
wherwith you begin, whether it be in a verse of sixe
syllables, eight, ten, twelve, etc. : and though this
precept might seem ridiculous unto you, since every
yong scholler can conceive that he ought to continue in
the same measure wherwith he beginneth, yet do I see
and read many mens Poems now adayes, whiche beginning with the measure of xij. in the first line, and xiiij.
in the second (which is the common kind of verse) they
wil yet (by that they have passed over a few verses) fal
into xiiij. and fourtene, et sic de similibus, the which is
either forgetfulnes or carelessnes.'[1] This was Skelton's
difficulty : when a new rhythm appeared under his pen,
so far from being reconciled with the metrical pattern
with which he had begun, it became dominant and superseded the original. And the truly ' balductum rhymes '
in Gabriel Harvey's Letterbook show that the habit of

[1] *Elizabethan Critical Essays*, I, 49.

consistency was not established in England, even among the learned, fifty years after Skelton's death.

The sonnet was a useful discipline to the court poets of the early century, but Wyatt's normal speech was not malleable enough to fit easily into the new form—that is, he was not rhetorician enough to make it fit. Others, down to Spenser's time, saved themselves from Skelton's chaos and Wyatt's cramp by keeping close to the metrical basis, the unvarying succession of accented and unaccented syllables with equally unvarying caesura. They could trust themselves only with the strictest pattern, because in their uncertain hands any indulgence in rhythmical variation was dangerous. ' Note you that commonly now a dayes in English rimes (for I dare' not cal them English verses) we use none other order but a foote of two sillables, whereof the first is depressed or made short, and the second is elevate or made long ; and that sound or scanning continueth throughout the verse.'[1] ' My meaning is, that all the wordes in your verse be so placed as the first sillable may sound short or be depressed, the second long or elevate, the third shorte, the fourth long, the fifth short, etc.'[2]

' There are also certayne pauses or rests in a verse, which may be called *Ceasures* . . . in mine opinion in a verse the pause will stand best in the middest, in a verse of tenne it will best be placed at the ende of the first foure sillables ; in a verse of twelve in the midst.'[3] Gascoigne regretted this bondage, which he knew to be a confession of weakness. ' We have used in times past other kindes of Meeters. . . . Also our father *Chaucer* hath used the same libertie in feete and measure that the Latin-

---

[1] *Elizabethan Critical Essays*, I, p. 50.
[2] *Ibid.*, p. 51. [3] *Ibid.*, p. 54.

ists do use. . . . And surely I can lament that wee
are fallen into suche a playne and simple manner of
wryting, that there is none other foote used but one.'
Within fifteen years the liberty was recovered, and
Spenser, though not alone, was foremost in its achievement.

However thick the fog round modern English metric,
it is clear enough that the metrical systems known to
Spenser would be three : the quantitative system of the
classics, the syllabic system of the French, and the system
of Chaucer, which, like all men of his time, he would
read as a somewhat irregular metre by omitting accented
final ' e's ' and anglicizing most of the French accentu-
ations. The contrast between the verse of Chaucer
and that of his followers would not be so noticeable
when they were read in this fashion, and the verse of
Langland would appear as a rougher, unrhymed but
heavily alliterated specimen of the Chaucerian method.
That is, Spenser would know that verse had been made
as a structure of long and short syllables, as a series of
lines each containing a fixed number of syllables and
bound together by rhyme, and as a series of lines each
containing a more or less fixed number of strong accents
more or less regularly disposed. These three systems
are very different, but they have in common the possibility of rhythmical variation—the Latin and the Chaucerian by the variation of the number of syllables in the
line, the French by variation in the disposition of the
accents. None of them provided a complete solution
of the difficulty of the English poets, for the syllables of
English vary within much wider limits than the classical
' long ' and ' short ' will serve to denote, even with the
destructive addition of Gascoigne's ' indifferent ' ; the

heavy accents of English require more regulation than the French system supplies ; and Chaucer's verse, as the sixteenth century read it, must have grated on the most pious ear. Spenser experimented with all three, and learned from each, until he arrived at something like Chaucer's compromise.

The one existing specimen of Spenser's Latin verse gives no high idea of his skill in the scholarly art, but the academic practice must have helped to develop his sense of metre, and when Sidney and Dyer succeeded (where Gabriel Harvey had failed [1]) in leading him to experiment in quantitative metres, that exercise was of still greater value. The whole episode is obscure, since only fragments have survived of what must have been long discussion and argument, but it seems that there were two schools in England. One, to which Harvey belonged, deriving from Alberti through Ascham, took the accent-value of a syllable as equivalent to its quantity, a system useful enough in Italian and English ; the other school followed a more elaborate code, observing position and other artificial devices. This system is more suitable for a lightly accented language like French, and indeed it seems like that of Baïf, whose Academy of Poetry and Music, in which the adaptation of quantitative metres was an avowed object, was in high favour just when Sidney was in Paris. [2] The argument between Spenser and Harvey turns on this difference in

---

[1] Though he still gets the credit of it, in spite of Spenser's perfectly clear statement : ' I am, of late, more in love with my Englishe versifying than with Ryming ; wyche I should have done long since, if I would then have followed your councell,' etc. (*Elizabethan Critical Essays*, I, p. 89). See also Sidney on verse, pp. 204–5.

[2] Of the ' Master Drant ' of Harvey's letters we know nothing to the point ; he may have only formulated the rules.

the method of measurement, and the value of the experiment lies in their discussion of the accentuation of certain
words, for the measuring of English syllables meant
wrestling with the English problem of accent and its
relation to certain other phenomena of speech-sounds.
The practice of Latin verse means practice in the placing
of words to the best advantage, in the best order, having
regard to style, significance, and rhythm : that is worth
learning, and indeed Spenser would find both Minturno
and Ronsard warning their readers to be careful of it.
The attempt to imitate Latin verse in English would
force Spenser's attention on the fact that the unit of
speech in English is not the word, but the phrase, that
since the relative position of words can be altered only
within very narrow limits, the phrase must be treated as
an indivisible whole, which it is in speech.   It is always
possible to explain that one has made a dactylic or a
spondaic line, and to call a necessary series of rapid
syllables a resolution, but the English writer must in
practice place to the best advantage not only words,
but phrases, must construct his metrical line out of longer
and less tractable rhythm-units than the Latin.

The French principle of syllabic regularity was observed, as we have seen, among Spenser's contemporaries,
and the heavier accent of English, regularized of necessity
along with the number of syllables, made dull and
monotonous verse. The poets of the Pléiade set an
example in variation of metre itself, and the imitation
of their lyric measures would not only enforce the lesson
of variety, but would teach the young poet how one line
is related to those before and after it, freeing him from
the tyranny of the line and teaching him to construct a
group of lines together.   In their critical works du Bellay

8

and Ronsard insist continually on the judgment of the
trained ear. 'Verses should be weighed, not counted,'
was, says Binet, one of Ronsard's maxims, and it was
the poet's ear that was to decide the disputed question of
licences—'having for that no rule more perfect than
your ear, which will never deceive you, if you will accept
its counsel with some judgment and reason '—' your
ear, which is the certain judge of the structure of verses.'[1]
From the French also he would learn that syllabic regularity is compatible with accentual variation, and in practice his ear would discover that the heavy accent of
English, making any variation more pronounced than
in French, restricts that variation considerably.[2]   Spenser's close imitation of Chaucer's verse in *The Shepheardes
Calender* was prompted, in all probability, more by some
notion of decorum than by a taste for metrical irregularity, but this motive also must have entered—if not when
he planned it, then as soon as he commenced work—
and in the experiment he would discover the limits of
irregularity permissible in a modern ear, and he might
well meditate on the significance of Gascoigne's remarks
on Chaucer's freedom. ' Our father *Chaucer* hath used
the same libertie in feete and measures that the Latinists
do use : and who so ever do peruse and well consider
his workes, he shall finde that although his lines are not
alwayes of one selfe same number of Syllables, yet, being
redde by one that hath understanding, the longest verse,
and that which hath most Syllables in it, will fall (to the
eare) correspondent unto that whiche hath fewest sillables

---

[1] *Art Poétique.*

[2] See, for example, the 7th stanza of the *November* Song, where the
movement changes (for no reason), while the number of syllables remains
as in other stanzas.

in it : and like wise that whiche hath in it fewest syllables shal be founde yet to consist of woordes that have
suche naturall sounde, as may seeme equall in length to a
verse which hath many moe sillables of lighter accentes.'[1]
That is, Gascoigne appeals from number to sound, from
metre to rhythm, but confesses that he and his contemporaries are unable to make verse on such principles.
This was the secret Spenser had to recover, the object of
his experiment.

In his study of Italian poetry Spenser would find
clearly expressed by Minturno the principle of time-
measurement. ' What is poetry ? Imitation[2] of divers
manners of persons, in various ways, either by words,
or by harmony, or by *tempi*, separately, or with all these
together, or with part of them.'[3] 'I call *tempi* those
measures and those intervals which are called *numbers*
by the Latins and *rhythms* by the Greeks, in songs, in
instrumental music, in speech, in dancing, in graceful
and apt movements of the body.'[4] 'Time (*tempo*) is the
measure of the movement of syllables and words, up to
the moment of their ending. And since movement is
slow or quick according to the space, long or short, during which it is made, time consists in the length and
shortness, and slowness and quickness, of the syllables
and words uttered.'[5] Here the principle of movement,
which is so closely related to style and sense, and which
is one of the most valuable lessons of Latin verse, is
definitely laid down, and when Minturno returns to the
subject later in his book he makes it follow on the dis-

---

[1] *Elizabethan Critical Essays*, I, p. 50.
[2] In the Aristotelian sense ; *Mimesis*, not to be confused with the
scholastic Imitation of an author.
[3] *L'Arte Poetica*, p. 2.   [4] P. 3.   [5] P. 13.

cussion of phrases and sentences and their arrangement
in verse, what E.K. called ' the knitting of sentences,
whych they call the joynts and members therof, and . . .
al the compasse of the speach.' ' Before we discuss the
tempi which we should use in verse, let us demonstrate
the manner of conjoining the divisions of speech, of
which there are three ways. The first depends on the
Articulations, as the Latin rhetoricians say, which by us
are called *joints* ; the second, on the members ; the
third on the compass (*circoito*), called by the Greeks the
Period. For a perfect speech, in which all its parts are to
be found, is like a spoken body, which has its members,
and in the members the joints. Thus as the members are parts of the compass, so the joints of the members.'[1]　That is, speech is divided into sentences, clauses,
and phrases, which last may consist of one word or of
several, but are always indivisible units. ' In this composition of words (*voci*) divided in three ways, consists
Harmony with the *tempi*, which are called *numbers* by
the Latins, rhythms by the Greeks.'[2]　Minturno pursues
the notions of harmony and number through soul,
body, movement, song, and instrumental music, showing that they consist in the relation of measurable units ;
and so in speech, long syllables being counted as twice
the length of short, they consist in the relation of the
intervals of time occupied by words and phrases when
they are spoken.

Minturno grows more vague as he proceeds in his
subject, and he seems little interested in the method of
counting by length of syllable. The important points
are his linking up of syntax and metre, and the idea of
time-measurement, with its natural corollary of judg-

---

[1] *L'Arte Poetica,* p. 353.　　　　[2] P. 354.

ment by ear—' Leaving aside this philosophy [the length
of syllables and the rule thereof], let us conclude that
since number is measure, or rather is subject to measure,
and without doubt is subject to the measure of the ears,
all that we estimate by their judgment, not only in
verse, but in prose also, is called Number. Hence, it
being born of the pleasure of the ear, in order that it
may delight, let it be used with certain measures of
delightful things, and with certain modes which are
defined and judged by the sense of hearing, not only in
all the verse, but in every part of the expression, whether
speech be distinguished by joints or divided into members or completed and rounded off in a compass.' [1]
Good verse, then, consists in so arranging the natural
rhythms of speech that the result may be pleasing to the
ear. For every grammatical phrase is a sound-rhythm
when it is spoken aloud, and every clause and every
sentence a more complex rhythm built up of the phrase-
units and the pauses between them. If this is related
to Gascoigne's idea of strict metre, then the double duty
of the modern poet is apparent : the reconciliation of
metrical pattern and the rhythm which is dictated by
the nature of the language.

It is obvious that all this is closely connected with
the nature of music, and indeed it is a striking fact—or
a profound problem—that the revival of English verse
coincides with the great age of English music. In this
very musical country poets had never ceased to achieve
in the singing voice the ease and perfection they failed
to accomplish in the speaking voice. The briefest comparison of Wyatt's songs with his sonnets gives sufficient
evidence. The more highly developed music of Eliza-

[1] *L'Arte Poetica*, p. 356. Cf. Cicero, *Orator*, 150, 164 ff.

bethan times was helpful in recognizing and organizing
the more complex rhythms of spoken verse, if only by
analogy, and the study and imitation of Italian and French
verse-forms and methods would be made easier by their
reinforcement in the musical settings which were im-
ported in great quantity. Music was so intimate a part
of the daily life of Elizabethan England that Spenser
could not fail to have his share of it. From youth his
ear would be trained by the ' noted ' services of the
Church, in which, as laid down by authority, each syllable
was sung to one tone.[1] Mulcaster's excellent scheme of
elementary education included, along with ' loud speaking,' singing and playing upon an instrument, and
Mulcaster himself contributed a commendatory Latin
poem—though indeed a dull and pedagogical composition which tells us nothing about his personal tastes
or interests—to the *Cantiones quae . . . Sacrae Vocantur*
of the aged Tallis and the younger and greater William
Byrd, published in 1575. Ronsard thought of verse
as essentially related to music : ' You will make your
verses masculine and feminine so far as you can, so as to
be more proper to music and the harmony of instruments,
in favour of which it seems that poetry was born ; for
poetry without the instruments, or without the grace of
a single voice or of several, is in no wise agreeable, any
more than the instruments unless they are animated by
the melody of a pleasant voice.'[2] ' Such verses are
marvellous proper for music, the lyre and other instruments ; and therefore when you call them Lyrics you
will not do wrong if now you lengthen and now shorten

---

[1] On the relation of musical tones to syllables, see an all too brief
letter from Mr. Stephen Gaselee, *T.L.S.*, 12th April, 1923.

[2] *Art Poétique*, p. 320.

them, and after a long line a short one, or two short, at the choice of your ear, keeping always as much as you can a good cadence of verse . . . for music and other instruments. . . . I would advise you also to speak your verses aloud when you make them, or rather sing them, whatever voice you have, for that is one of the principal things, which you must observe most carefully.'[1]

Ronsard here gives the practical reason of ' broken and cuttit ' lyrical verse, but the ' contaminatio ' of music with verse was of use even in other forms. In the first place, since music is essentially formal, it helped to abolish Skeltonic doggerel. In the second, it broke the tyranny of rigid metre and assisted the establishment of free rhythm. The modern application of musical mechanism to the construction of verse consists in replacing the metrical scheme by a time-signature and the feet by bars, but it must be remembered that neither of these inventions was known to Elizabethan music. If, then, we consider music in relation to Elizabethan verse we must divest ourselves of the notion of equal barring and the regular accent it suggests, and think only of a sequence of free (but related) rhythms, whose form is not controlled in advance by a time-signature, but has to be recognized by the executant as he sings or plays. This is possible in music because the notes of which the phrase is made up are exactly measurable —one breve equalling two semibreves, one semibreve two minims, and so on—so that the form of the rhythms and their relation one to another are easily recognized by the ear. The absence of strict time forced the musician's attention on his rhythms, on each as a separate unit in his construction and on their relation to one

[1] *Ibid.*, p. 332.

another in form—that is, in length and movement—so that his sequence of rhythms might be built into a logical and coherent whole. Thus also every singer, which means every educated man of that happy time, had his ear for rhythm strengthened by the practice of music, the more that that music was polyphonic, so that every rhythm had to be related not only to those before and after in sequence, but to other, and often very different or even contrasting rhythms accompanying it. We may, therefore, estimate the distance which separates the simple prosody of Gascoigne, not only from the freedom of Virgil or Chaucer, but also from the complexity of the madrigal, and we may be permitted to imagine that Spenser, with a certain training in music and considerable practice in the weighing and measuring of syllables, learned from the musician that the ear is able to contain the whole sum of a rhythm, and to compare and contrast it with others both in sequence and together. Music thus assisted in forming the conception of verse as a sequence of variable rhythms, whose variation is controlled and whose relation is preserved by constant reference to a strict pattern, which we call the metre. The reference to the metre might be expressed in musical terms thus, that the poet constructs his sequence of variable rhythms in relation to the metre, and that Spenser was enabled to do this freely because he was accustomed to counterpoint even more than to harmony ; or thus, that the metre is an implied or silent ground bass over which the poet plays a descant.

This notion of a relationship between music and verse is but reinforced when it is considered that Elizabethan music was largely for the voice, and based thus on speech. The musical rhythms conformed normally to the natural rhythms of English—that is, to the rhythms imposed by English syntax and vocabulary. Thus the poet, however strictly he might try to keep to his metre, would find the syntactical, non-metrical rhythms of his verse thrown into relief, developed and emphasized by the musician who set his poem after a method he had learned from Italian and French masters, and so he would acquire the habit of considering the sound of his poem as a rhythmical as well as a metrical composition. When poet and musician worked in such close co-operation each was bound to have regard to the other's medium—the poet to ' keep a good cadence ' and a pleasant variety, and the musician to bring out the meaning of the words. The lesson is easily carried over from song to other poetical forms, especially in an intensely musical age and country. For in England the singing verse frequently predominates in poetry ; the average English ear prefers Spenser to Donne, Tennyson to Browning, and fails to appreciate French poetry, because the Englishman hears in song and not in speech. That is why in England blank verse is the mode of poetry intended or supposed to be spoken. Rhyme often betrayed the young Shakespeare into song when he did not mean it, and it was only after a generation of professional acting had trained an English ear to the lighter and more varied movement of the speaking voice that a Ben Jonson could complain to King James that ' his master, Mr. G. Buchanan, had corrupted his eare when young, and learned him to sing verses when he sould have read them.'[1]

Music has this virtue also, that it measures pauses as well as tones. It is the measurable pause that links one

[1] Conversations with Drummond of Hawthornden.

musical phrase to another. The ear may continue a rhythm from one phrase to another through a pause, recognizing that they are articulations of the same member, or a pause may be so long as to let the ear perceive that one member is complete and another about to begin. In metre, the pauses are the caesura and the line-ending ; in speech, they fall between phrases, clauses, and sentences, and the poet must decide which is to predominate and control the other. The unskilful Gascoigne and the supremely skilful Pope make the rhythm of their speech fit into the metre ; the poets whose ear is tuned to the voice of the actor, and still more those like Spenser and Milton, whose ear is trained to appreciate the variable rhythms of Elizabethan music in all its contrapuntal subtlety, observe the more measurable pauses of natural speech. They vary the position of the caesura within the line, and they often use the line-ending merely as a lighter pause through which a rhythm may be continued. The varied fall of the pauses is one of the beauties of *Paradise Lost*, and so it is of *The Faerie Queene*. The stanzaic form requires that variety, and, since the infinite variation of natural speech is more difficult to reproduce in rhymed stanza than in blank verse, it must be constructed, if it is not to become intolerably monotonous, on a principle very closely analogous to that of music. The poet has to learn to preserve the form of his stanza, and yet to make, within that form, a new form, varying from stanza to stanza, built up of the units of speech which are also units of rhythm, and pleasantly agreeing or contrasting with the strict metrical form of the pattern stanza.

In this endeavour music and rhetoric meet and coalesce. In the practice of ' numerous ' prose, which Spenser would labour over in his Ciceronian studies, he would learn to organize the rhythms of speech, and the practice would assist when he came to the more complete and exacting organization of speech-rhythms in verse. Much of rhetoric is concerned with sound, as every writer knows. The sequence of vowels and consonants, their phonetic relations, are as important in the creation of pleasant or suggestive sound as the length and movement of rhythms. Thus when critics write of the 'music' of Spenser's verse they usually mean the sweet fluid sequences of identical or closely-related vowel-sounds linked by simple consonants, but that charm— one of the most easily recognized of Spenser's characteristics—is only a part of musical utterance, timbre, or tone. The point may be studied in Dryden's St. Cecilia Ode : it is his rhetorical skill that Dryden exploits in his endeavour to suggest the timbre of the different musical instruments. Nor is it merely the elements of rhythm and tone, though they are the most important, that rhetoric and music have in common. The 'figures of arrangement' are common to both, the inversions, the repetitions. William Byrd might have written a stanza like this :

> So down he fell, and forth his life did breath,
> That vanisht into smoke and cloudes swift ;
> So downe he fell, that th' earth him underneath
> Did grone, as feeble so great load to lift ;
> So downe he fell, as an huge rocky clift,
> Whose false foundation waves have washt away,
> With dreadful poyse is from the mayneland rift,
> And rolling downe great Neptune doth dismay :
> So downe he fell, and like an heaped mountain lay

By force of rhetorical arrangement Spenser makes more lyrical than its original the passage he borrowed from Tasso in the last Canto of the Fourth Book, and where he seems most dilatory he is often merely playing with, restating and developing a theme throughout a stanza.   Most of all it may be remarked in the close of his stanza, where the rhythm of the last line may be brought to a full close as in the stanza quoted above, or suspended by a lightly-rhythmed phrase which leads on to the opening of the next stanza, and between the various passages of a Canto, where the whole of the last stanza of an episode is slowly brought to a definite ending and the first stanza of the new passage opened on a new and contrasting rhythm :

> And on his warlike beast them both did beare,
> Himselfe by them on foot to succour them from feare.

> So when that forrest they had passed well . . .

The crisp series of short words is typical of Spenser's method of opening.   The whole question of the relation of stanza to stanza is worthy of observation, and it may be noted that the method may be expressed in terms of rhetoric or of music ; for the two are one.   Style and verse cannot be considered apart unless in the abstract. By his recognition of this close relationship and his achievement of the skill to make them work together under control for his own purposes, Spenser improved both and taught future English poets to write.

CHAPTER V

Imitation ; Matter ; Allegory

The suggestion of musical form in Spenser's poetry is not always fortuitous, or even to be traced so far back as the fundamental unity of the arts or the essential similarity of their expressive devices. It is often intentional, for Spenser would certainly hold the common Aristotelian theory of art, that art is Mimesis, imitation. Poetry is ' Imitation of divers manners of persons, in various ways, either by words or by harmony or by numbers, separately, or by all these together. . . . Diverse again are the things with which Imitation is accomplished. For painters accomplish it with colours and lines, parasites and actors with voice and action, poets, as I have said, with words, with harmony, and with numbers.'[1] The ' blending of sound and sense ' was more than an added charm of poetry ; it was its very foundation as art, and the principle of unity among the diverse elements of the poet's medium. Thus when Spenser has occasion to tell of music he uses his rhetorical skill to reproduce musical form.

> The joyous birdes, shrouded in chearefull shade
> Their notes unto the voice attempred sweet ;
> Th' Angelicall soft trembling voyces made
> To th' instruments divine respondence meet ;

---

[1] Minturno, *L'Arte Poetica*, pp. 2–3.

> The silver sounding instruments did meet
> With the base murmure of the waters fall ;
> The waters fall with difference discreet,
> Now soft, now loud, unto the wind did call ;
> The gentle warbling wind low answered to all.[1]

That is an admirable example of skill in the use of the rhetorical device of repetition with augmentation ; it might also be described as an example of development of successive themes on repetition ; most of all it is a brilliant transference into words of the effect of polyphonic music. If, say, Weelkes had set music to that stanza, he might have reduplicated the effect, but he would not have altered it, for Spenser has already suggested, by choice of words, by the fall of rhythms, and by the figure of augmented repetition, the entry of different voices in counterpoint and harmony. Let it be repeated that this is intentional, an example of Mimesis. It is a more complex creation than the suggestion of hoarse noise in such a stanza as this :

> He cryde, as raging seas are wont to rore
> When wintry storme his wrathful wreck does threat ;
> The rolling billows beat the ragged shore,
> As they the earth would shoulder from her seat ;
> And greedy gulfe does gape, as he would eat
> His neighbour element in his revenge :
> Then gin the blustring brethren boldly threat,
> To move the world from off his stedfast henge,
> And boisterous battaile make, each other to avenge.[2]

And it is more successful, partly because Spenser had more gift that way, partly, perhaps, because he spent more loving care on the suggestion of art, partly because in imitating beautiful sound he always thought in terms

---

[1] Book II, xii, 72.   [2] Book I, xi, 21.

of music, whose organized rhythms could be reproduced
by the organization of his own very conscious speech-
rhythms in the forms of rhetoric.

Poetry, however, is more than organized sound ; it
must appeal to all the senses, and, as sight is the quickest
and most used of all the five, the theory of Mimesis
received very early and very naturally an expression in
pictorial terms. *Ut pictura poesis.* ' Poesie . . . is an
arte of imitation, for so *Aristotle* termeth it in his word
Mimesis, that is to say, a representation, counterfetting,
or figuring forth : to speake metaphorically, a speaking
picture.'[1] Spenser also made his speaking picture or
picture in speech. The old lady who, when Pope read
to her from *The Faerie Queene*, said he had been showing
her a gallery of pictures, indeed ' said very right,'[2] and the
pictorial sense, like the musical, was innate in Spenser
and was also cultivated for his purposes in poetry. The
symbolic figures of the months are, as Ruskin showed,
the traditional figures illuminated in mediaeval Books
of Hours,[3] and the reader is reminded often, in such
passages as the Masque of Cupid,[4] not only of court
masques which Spenser may have seen, but of the wood-
cuts of the *Hypnerotomachia Poliphili* and those in the
old editions of Petrarch's *Trionfi*. *The Shepheardes
Calender* is adorned with cuts of a not indecorous
crudity ; the *Dreames* also were to be illustrated,[5] and
the highly decorative St. George in *The Faerie Queene*

---

[1] Sidney, *Apologie for Poetrie* ; *Elizabethan Critical Essays*, I, 158.
See also Mr. Gregory Smith's note on this passage.

[2] Spence's *Anecdotes.*

[3] Book VII, vii ; Ruskin, *Stones of Venice*, Vol. II, vii, §§ 52–3.

[4] Book III, xii.

[5] Postscript to Spenser's second letter to Harvey, Globe edition, p. 709.

testifies that the taste survived Spenser's translation to Ireland.

The description of personages in small space and in colours may be referred to the study of illuminated manuscripts ; it comes also from the poetry of the same age as the manuscripts, from Chaucer and Lidgate ; these were alike available to Spenser, and poetry and painting could be studied together. England had not yet produced much engraving, and that not great, but there were, as has been observed, excellent Italian and French works, some of which he must have known, and the absence of definite colour-notes in the Masque of Cupid suggests engraving rather than painting. More influential than these in the training of the poet's eye must have been the English, French, and Flemish tapestries with which great houses were decorated—tapestries such as those he describes so lavishly as adorning the house of Busyrane,[1] and the occasional formality of Spenser's figures, and still more the decorative accessories of flowers and animals, suggest the fanciful rigidity of design in ' costly clothes of Arras and of Toure.' Even discounting the literary precedents on which Spenser was working, this need not be considered strange. Our mode of vision is imposed on most of us by the art we know ; we learn to see colour and composition from the painters, and our mental images, the creation of which is part of the painter's own activity, are normally affected by the memory of pictures as much as by the memory of nature. Spenser had the pictorial sense strongly developed : that is, he discriminated and organized his seeing as he did his hearing, and just as the musician assisted, so did the painter, the engraver, the tapestry-maker.

[1] Book III, xi.

Thus, even when he was not describing a work of art, he was 'imitating' what he saw in his mind, and that might well be, even though he was scarcely conscious of it, an Italian wood-engraving, an English illumination, a Beauvais tapestry ; at least it was such a mental image as an artist in one or other of these kinds might visualize as he thought over a new design. The gift was there, it was developed by the art he knew, and the deliberate cultivation of the imagination in pictorial vision was encouraged by the common theory of the critics.

In the postscript in which he reports to Harvey the progress of the *Dreames*, Spenser mentions Michael Angelo, but he must have known that master only by reputation. What works of the Italian painters he did see cannot even be conjectured, but probably there was little to be seen in England before 1581, the date of his going to Ireland. If the contemplated journey to France, which was discussed in Harvey's correspondence, was ever accomplished, it would provide some opportunities in the collections of Francis I and his descendants, and Spenser's eye, like Ronsard's, may have owed some of its mode of vision to the Clouets, to Primaticcio and the school of Fontainebleau. This is as may be, but in any case the unity of the Renaissance is curiously exemplified by the affinity of Spenser's work with that of the great painters of the Continent, and his pictorial capacity generally by comparison with the great painters of any age. Without suggesting the dangerous practice of book illustration, innumerable pleasant coincidences might be indulged. Carpaccio, one imagines, would have enjoyed the Red Cross Knight's battle with the Dragon—more, for instance, than would Raphael, though he also painted his St. George. Jean Fouquet

9

would appreciate a brightness and precision like his own, Paolo Uccello the quality at once decorative and intense of these fights and meetings in the solemn woodlands, and Michael Angelo himself, painter, sculptor, poet, and critic, might find something to admire in the figures round the gates of Death and in the council of the Gods. Before many, Botticelli, compact like Spenser of imagination and intellect, painter of myth and of religion, might perceive something of his own in the vision of Belphœbe, issuing from among the trees, her purfled garments flowing,

> And whether art it were, or heedlesse hap,
> As through the flouring forrest rash she fled,
> In her rude haires sweet flowres themselves did lap,
> And flourishing fresh leaves and blossomes did enwrap.[1]

And, set to paint the symbolic Dragon lying dead, Lippo Lippi or Masaccio could not have failed to show the city towers in the background with the watchman on the wall, nor have omitted, alongside the ceremonial procession that comes from the gates, the crowd of burgher folk, the adventurous boys, the frightened children and their mothers. That is a matter of imagination ; in purely pictorial quality, the poetic master of *chiaroscuro* could not but please the painters who have loved the play of light. It is not surprising to find Turner trying to express in his medium the physical character of *The Faerie Queene*, and in the memory of Rembrandt, had he known it, the phrase might have lingered :

> his glistering armor made
> A little glooming light, much like a shade.[2]

---

[1] Book II, iii, 21–30.   [2] Book I, i, 14.

This pleasant pastime is not entirely frivolous, for it enforces appreciation not only of the artistic power of Spenser, but of his wonderful variety. Hazlitt was surely too much a slave to the fashion of his time when he said that ' Nobody but Rubens could have painted the fancy of Spenser,' however truly he adds that ' he could not have given the sentiment, the airy dream, that hovers over it.' [1] Rubens has his place indeed, but only as one of many, from the mediaeval masters of illumination down through all the line of the Renaissance, through all who preserved the freshness of romance and achieved the classical security, to Claude Lorraine, and so while the pictorial sense endures. Here, as in other ways, the poet who came last into the field gathers up, as no other artist in any medium has done, a whole phase of the Renaissance.

This theory of Imitation has been distinguished from the pedagogic method of the humanists, but the line must not be drawn too strictly. For the Renaissance poet the sum of the universe included the poems men had written as well as the things they were written about, and if he might claim help in his imitation from the other arts, surely he might from his own. A phrase of Virgil, an episode from Ariosto, were as much his to use as the colour of a rose or the brightness of sunshine ; a man may find a story in Plato or Plutarch as full of human significance as a tramp's gossip or the report of a murder trial. Man's intellect is the greatest work of God, and surely its workings are as noble poetic stuff as those of the blind forces of matter. Any artist must use figures, images, external things, to express what he wishes to express, or be content to remain unintelligible to his

[1] Lectures on the English Poets : Spenser

fellow-men for lack of common ground of understanding. He awakens feeling by evoking its causes, and, naturally, since it is first of all his own feelings that are in question, he uses the images that have emotional value for himself, that mean most to himself. And if a poet love books, what harm ? Spenser might object with du Bellay to the servility of the latinists, ' building their poems out of the hemistiches of Virgil and swearing in their proses by the words and sentences of Cicero,'[1] but he might continue, in speaking of his own vernacular poems, ' Let there appear no verse, wherein appears not some vestige of rare and antique erudition.'[2] The new poets were scholars, and proud of it. They wrote for scholars who would understand and appreciate the neat insetting of a well-known phrase to enrich the content of a passage by the reader's memory of its origin, and still more, perhaps, of a ' sentence,' the sententious saying which that age so loved and studied in the classics and in the collections of Erasmus and Stephanus.

The ' imitation ' of an author, however, meant much more than casual quotation. ' This *Imitatio* is *similis materiei dissimilis tractatio* and, also, *dissimilis materiei similis tractatio*.'[3] The ancients taught the modern age, as we have seen, how poetry should be written ; they gave also the matter of poetry. Whole passages were borrowed for new purposes, from the classics and the Italians especially. It is translation on the fragmentary scale, old matter turned to a new aspect, or a variation on a well-known theme. There are themes so common as almost to be regarded as test pieces—the list of trees

---

[1] *Deff. et Ill.*, p. 91. [2] *Ibid.*, p. 114.
[3] Ascham, *Scholemaster*, in *Eliz. Crit. Essays*, I, 8.

which descended from Ovid through Statius and Chaucer, the catalogue of flowers translated in *Virgils Gnat* and imitated in *Muiopotmos*, and a dozen Latin and Italian others. Normally, again, the poet is conscious of his succession, conscious that he is writing of things which elder and perhaps better poets have treated, and he remembers, even when he does not deliberately imitate, their *tractatio*. Thus in *Colin Clouts Come Home Again*, for instance,—and the same process may be observed in all his work—Spenser was treating of actual people and actual happenings in his own life, and at the same time, even discounting the pastoral scheme, every episode in the poem is a well-known theme of poetry. The meeting of the poets, the Ovidian horror of the sea, the panegyric upon a monarch, the courteous commemoration of friends and brother-poets, the attack on court life, the celebration of a mistress—in all these passages literary and personal motives and interests are inextricably bound up together ; and we must accept them together and try to appreciate both at the same time, or we shall miss something he meant us to see and enjoy. Like any other artist, Spenser made his art express the interests and feelings of his life, and exercised his art upon the universe he knew, keeping the two converse activities balanced. And books were a loved part of his life, of his universe.

The same complete fusion of interests causes the endless dispute about the ' sincerity ' of the love-sonnets of Spenser as of every other sonnetteer. The argument is an unconscious recognition that the sonnet is one of the perfect forms for the expression of personal emotion, and that by Renaissance convention the poet was permitted to ' imitate ' his personal emotions in that form :

such is the specific usage of the sonnet 'kind.' Even in the sonnet, however, the habit of the Renaissance prevailed. When the Petrarchan sonnet was revived by the school of Bembo, and so carried over all Europe, a mediaeval survival, on the flood of humanism, the prestige of its sponsors added it to the stock of respectable 'kinds,' and by the same token the virtue of a sonnet sequence as imitation was as important in the eyes of its author and its admirers as its virtue as expression—or rather, as is suggested above, no distinction can justly be drawn. The passionate cry of Catullus is scarcely heard in the North until Donne revolted against the whole convention. So plain-spoken a mode of address conflicted with the lingering habit of secrecy enjoined by the mediaeval code, the habit which made artificial the courteous love-poetry of chivalry, and classicism joined with this aristocratic reserve made a veil of imitation welcome. It was a question also of literary ethics : morality is not an æsthetic consideration, perhaps, but the artist is a citizen and responsible for the effect of his works on others ; so also the poet is a man, but he is responsible to the Muses that his works have artistic value apart from their value as the expression of his own feelings. So men wrote love-sonnets in imitation of the master of the love-sonnet, just as they wrote epics in imitation of the master of Epic. And after all, if a man regards Petrarch as the best writer of love-poems, and has been brought up to copy the best writers, it would be a poor compliment to his lady to address her in any other mode. Critics may divide sonnets into categories of 'sincere' and 'insincere' ; it is safer, as well as easier, to divide them into 'good' and 'bad.' The appearance of sincerity may be due to greater skill, and the stupidest imitation may cloak the dumbness of the sincerest lover.

> So when my toung would speak her praises dew
> it stopped is with thoughts astonishment :
> and when my pen would write her titles true
> it ravisht is with fancies wonderment [1]—

a universal experience of lovers, ' imitated ' by Spenser from the sixteenth and thirty-second sonnets of Petrarch, or from some other of the ten-score who imitated them, and as old as the *Romance of the Rose.*

Petrarchism was in the first place a mode of feeling. The emotional poetry of the troubadours had been transmuted by the poets of Bologna and Florence into mystical philosophy more subtly and more completely than in the North, where scholastic instruction lies in unassimilated strata among the eroticism of the *Romance of the Rose.* The originality of Petrarch was his perfect fusion or nice balance of the intellectual and the emotional, for Dante's desire for Beatrice dissolved in intellect, but Petrarch raised his love to a pitch of ecstasy without losing its humanity : if, as some of his contemporaries alleged, Laura was only an ideal, she was an ideal woman and not a metaphysical abstraction. When it was an adopted attitude, and no longer the real experience it was to Petrarch, the Petrarchan feeling became a somewhat vague and tenuous sentiment. As such it was not entirely to the robust taste of Ronsard any more than the ' platonic love ' with which it was often allied, and when in a few sonnets Spenser strayed out of the Petrarchan circle, it was in company with Ronsard and Ronsard's neo-Latin models rather than with any other sonnetteer of the

---

[1] *Amoretti*, iii.

century.   But the mode of sentiment is not all, or even
the greatest part of the matter commonly borrowed from
Petrarch.   Like the sardonic disillusionment of Byron
in a later age (though for purely mechanical reasons more
slowly) the despair and hope and joy and revulsion of
Petrarch were absorbed into the temperament of all
Europe.   The story of Petrarch and Laura, the world-
old and permanently attractive tale of a hopeless love
which was the framework of the *Rime*, prescribed the
general attitude of future actors, the situations and the
decorative detail were borrowed and rearranged by
sonnetteers from Spain to Scotland.   The sense of
exile and the feeling of the sympathy of nature that is
one of the fruits of loneliness, constant in Petrarch,
became constant in the poetry of the whole century.

Any tabulation of borrowings must be tentative, by
reason of the very community of much of the matter
borrowed.   ' Few, but they be well sented, can trace
him out '—no single original can be found for any given
sonnet.   Thus Spenser is not a ' Petrarchist ' like Wyatt
or Surrey—or is the more a Petrarchist ; he borrows less
obviously than du Bellay, and most like Ronsard, lavishly,
but widely.   No one man was his master, for though
Petrarch was the head fountain, yet the actual stuff of the
Amoretti and of the amatory eclogues may come from
Ariosto, from Tasso, Sannazaro, Tebaldeo, Bembo, from
Anthologies such as those collections of *Rime* published
by Giolito of Venice, from Marot, Ronsard, Desportes,
a score of others, or may have been used precisely because
all of them had used it.   Spenser assimilated his reading
thoroughly.   Thought, situation, ornament, the point of
cleverness that attracted men to Petrarch and often ruined
their taste, might be borrowed, but rarely all three to-

gether. The *similis materies* of the certainty of poetic
fame receives the *dissimilis tractatio* of ' One day I wrote
her name upon the strand ' ; Petrarch's trick of playing
upon his lady's name reappears in ' Most happy letters
framd by skilful trade ' and those curious puns on ' Peace '
—some of them actual quotations from Petrarch—pointed
out recently by Mr. Garrod.[1] In such a complication
of interests it is extremely difficult to decide whether
the motive is personal or literary—whether any particular
sonnet has biographical significance or is but another
example of sixteenth-century fashion.   Among the *Amoretti* we find the Sonnet Written in His Sickness, the Cruel
Letter, the Calumny—all to be paralleled from almost
any sonnet sequence Italian, French, or English—but
there is no sonnet To His Lady Weeping, or To His
Lady When She Was Sick ; and who can tell whether
it is accident or design ?   The incidents might happen
to anybody, or they might not.   The conditions of publication make it impossible to decide whether the series
is complete and final, and the printer's arrangement
leaves the relation between the Sonnets, the Epigrams,
and the *Epithalamion* obscure.   Were they to be read
as one sequence, or as separate and distinct ?   Does the
collection tell us the incomplete story of Spenser's wooing
of Elizabeth Boyle, widow of Tristram Peace, or the whole
story, as suggested by Mr. Long,[2] of an unsuccessful
wooing of Lady Carey ?   Or is this but another Petrarchan tale ?   The point is important only to biographers.
There were several ladies to whom Spenser might have
written sonnets, the Rosalind of *The Shepheardes Calender*,
the *altera Rosalindula, corculum meum*, of the Harvey

---

[1] *Times Literary Supplement*, 10th and 24th May, 1923.
[2] *Modern Language Review*, III (1908).

correspondence, Elizabeth Boyle, Lady Carey, and possible others might be addressed in terms of gallantry, of *amour courtois*. An accidental discovery shows that the first sonnet originally dedicated, not the *Amoretti*, but a copy of *The Faerie Queene* [1] ; the *Amoretti* may well be a collection of Sonnets On Several Occasions. There is again the intermediate emotion, a nameless and undefined æsthetic experience recognized as love—as in other circumstances it might be fear or joy—translated into terms of love as the nearest equivalent for the purpose of expression. It was called for, also, that the Prince of Poets should prove himself capable of a sonnet-sequence, since every young poet in London was busy with the numbers Petrarch flowed in ; even in Ireland, Spenser could not be out of the fashion.

There we may leave the question. Artistic sincerity is not to be confused with truth to fact. The one certain fact is the literary fact, and to us the rest is of very minor importance, as Spenser and his contemporaries probably saw when they refused to make their works any more explicit than they are. The problem of the *Amoretti*, as of Shakespeare's Sonnets, is a problem because the facts necessary to its elucidation were known to those in the author's immediate circle, or perhaps only to those immediately concerned ; as for others, and as for posterity, they were not of the circle, not concerned in the personal bearing of the affair, and they might take the poems as they found them, as works of art. It is scarcely in human nature to be so completely disinterested, but we must recognize the purely literary motive intertwined with the personal. The limiting cases are *Virgils Gnat* and *Epithalamion*. Without the dedicatory prologue,

[1] Gollancz : *Proceedings of the British Academy*, 1908.

no one would suspect that a version of Virgil's *Culex* had
a personal bearing, was a move in an actual event of
Spenser's life—an event which apparently caused him
considerable emotion ; and even apart from the *coda*
which explains that the *Epithalamion* was a gift from bride-
groom to bride, no one has ever dreamed of suggesting
that it is a mere literary exercise, or aught but the purest
and fullest wellspring of rich emotion in the English
language. Yet it is an obvious and deliberate imitation
of the Marriage-Songs of Catullus—the most elaborate,
least passionate of his poems—modelled as to its form
on the *canzoni* of Petrarch. If the *Epithalamion* proves
anything, it proves that humanist method was not so
barren as might appear. The humanists' lessons could
not make bad poetry any more necessarily than they
could make good poetry : it is the poet that makes the
difference. They taught Spenser to study and imitate
Latin poems ; the Italian critics, to study and imitate
Italian ; the French—it was the solvent addition—to
imitate both and to remember he was English. Spenser, born and trained for poetry, saw the relation between
marriage-ode and love-canzone, fused them together,
and knew enough, had skill enough, and had poetic force
enough, to make this out of them.

It is not to the present purpose to tabulate Spenser's
borrowings—that has provided and will continue to provide scholarly amusement for many a year—but the fact
of their existence and the reasons behind it must be understood, and a very little study serves to show the width
of Spenser's interests and the freedom of his methods.
Mother Hubberds Tale may have grown out of Spenser's
disappointment with slow and scanty preferment, and it
is a satire on certain social and political conditions of his

time ; it also includes pictures of the good and the bad
courtier, and it is a continuation of a native literary
tradition. Sir Thomas More, to go no farther back,
used the same method in his prose : ' My mother had
(when I was a lyttle boy) a good old woman that tooke
heede to her chyldren ; they called her mother Mawde.
. . . She was wont when shee sat by the fire wyth us,
to tell us, that were children, many childysh tales. . . .
I remember me that among other of her fond tales, she
told us once, that the Asse and the Wolfe came upon
a tyme to confession to the Foxe. . . .'[1]   So also Wyatt
tells how

> My mothers maides when they do sewe and spinne
> They sing a song made of the feldishe mouse. . . .

And we may be sure that Spenser's writing in the same
vein was deliberate, that he was aware that men would
link up his fable with others they knew, and intended
that they should. His most ' occasional ' poems have
their literary side, and in those he wrote ' for himself
and his Muses,' through all his working life from *The
Shepheardes Calender* to *The Faerie Queene*, the same
variety of reading and imitation is evident, along with
the same variety of motive and interest. The reason
for the choice of Arthur as hero of Spenser's romantic
epic has already been noticed. Any Englishman who
wrote on the subject of Arthur must found his work upon
Malory's. Virgil and Homer were the masters of epic,
Ariosto had set a new model of romance, and after Spenser
had begun, the *Gerusalemme Liberata* of Tasso appeared,
a further spur to emulation and an example of just that

---

[1] *A Dyalogue of Comforte* ; *Works*, ed. of 1557, p. 1183.

fusion of interests—moral allegory couched in a form reconciling epic and romance—which Spenser himself had plotted. It is not surprising, then, to find in *The Faerie Queene* much of Malory, much of Tasso, something of Virgil and Homer, a great deal of Ariosto, and many fragments which may come from more than one, re-borrowings of borrowings. In imitating these authors, and with them Chaucer, Spenser was as well justified in his own eyes as a modern scientist who utilizes the work of predecessors in the building up of his own.

These, however, by no means exhaust the list of Spenser's creditors ; if they did, Spenser would be a lesser poet. It was the width of his reading, the number of his creditors, and his own taste and cunning to select and fit together, that saved Spenser both from rigidity and from losing his individuality. He was the poet of scholarship, of romance and epic, but he was not ashamed of the homely fables of his own land. The Pléiade, his best masters, taught the doctrine of imitation, but they did not teach a doctrine of the imitation of any one master, and so they were free men, and Spenser their pupil was free with them, as, in practice if not in theory, neither latinist nor Bembist was free. They were not slaves ploughing a master's field, but lawful heirs enjoying an inheritance of many harvests. They took what they would with a high hand. Ascham states the humanist position well enough : ' The second kind of *Imitation* is to folow for learning of tonges and sciences the best authors. Here riseth . . . a great controversie, whether one or many are to be folowed. . . .'[1] ' Now to returne to that Question, whether one, a few, many, or all are to be followed, my aunswere shalbe short : All, for him

[1] *Scholemaster* ; *Elizabethan Critical Essays*, I, p. 7.

that is desirous to know all. . . . . But in everye separate kinde of learnyng, and studie by it selfe, ye must follow closelie a few, and chiefly some one, and that namelie in our schole of eloquence, either for penne or talke.'[1] The first duty of the imitator was to choose a model suitable to his subject, the second, to keep to that model. But the new poets had many purposes to serve in their great poems ; they imitated many models, and though they did not imitate at random, they sought variety to consort with their variety of subject.

Reasons for the selection of any passages borrowed for insertion into the work are as various as the sources. The kind of *The Faerie Queene*, as has been noticed, inevitably led to borrowing, since the foundation of it had to be recognizable, ' made famous by many men's former writings,' and by all the critical rules it had to be enlivened with ' episodes,' which, naturally, had to be of the correct Ariostian or Virgilian, romantic or epic kind. Certain borrowings may appear in the poem because critical convention prescribed them, some for their beauty, some because their subjects were fashionable at the time, some as evidences of scholarship, some for the teaching they embodied, and so on. Here as everywhere, of course, motives converge. Britomart's recognition of Arthegall after their fight in the sixth canto of Book IV, for instance, probably came largely from the *Morte Darthur* of Malory, Book IV, chapter xviii. It is a stock incident in romance —there are several other examples in Malory alone— it is also a capital instance of ' agnition,' a critical point taken over from Aristotle's discussion of tragedy into epic and so into romantic criticism : ' Agnition is the passing over from not knowing a thing at first to knowing

[1] *Ibid.*, p. 22.

it afterwards ' [1]—legislation after the fact, and a piece of pure pedantry, but the kind of thing Spenser and his contemporaries were nurtured on. The mythological vision in the tenth canto of the Sixth Book has many personal references, also imitations of Ovid and Claudian, and matter from Hesiod ; it is a supreme example of Renaissance picture-making, and it gives another turn to the treatment of Courtesy by an exposition of the meaning of the Graces, taken from Servius's commentary on Virgil or from Boccaccio's dictionary of mythology, and altered to convey a more Christian doctrine. One all-embracing reason there is for the appearance of a borrowed phrase or episode, and that is that Spenser liked it, and coveted it for himself, for his poem, and for England.

As the master of English poetry, ' well of English un-defiled,' Chaucer was a source of language and style rather than of matter. To re-versify him would be to fall into the error of the latinists ; and Spenser took over only what Chaucer had left unfinished, the Squire's tale on which he intended to found the Fourth Book of *The Faerie Queene,* or what Chaucer had in common with others, the symbolism of *The Romance of the Rose* and the mythology of the Court of Cupid which grew out of Ovid and could be found in Marot. The time had not yet come for modernizing Chaucer, and Spenser saw the virtues of his master of craft too clearly to think of improving him. Nothing, then, was to be gained by close imitation, and something might be lost. ' Indeed, just as it is in no wise a vice, but highly laudable, to borrow from a foreign language sentences and words, and appropriate them to one's own, so it is greatly repre-

[1] Pigna, *I Romanzi,* p. 27 ; Aristotle, *Poetics,* xi. 2.

hensible, not to say odious to every liberal-minded reader, to see Imitation in the same language as that, even, of some scholars, who think themselves the better the more they resemble a Heroet or a Marot.   I admonish you therefore (you who desire the enlargement of your tongue and wish to excel in it) not to imitate lightly . . . the most famous authors of that language, as do usually the greater part of our French poets—a thing surely vicious, being of no profit to our vernacular, since it is nothing other (O great liberality !) than to give her what was her own. I should like our language to be so rich in home examples that we need not have recourse to foreigners.   But if Virgil and Cicero had been content to imitate those of their own tongue, what would the Latins have, beyond Ennius or Lucretius, beyond Crassus or Antonius ? '[1] Something had to be made of borrowed matter ; it had to be transformed in being turned to a new use.   The master's work could not be rehandled, because it was already in masterly form, but foreign poetry could be made new, and made Spenser's, by making it English ; the doggerel *Bevis of Hamptons* could be used, because any value they had could be turned to better account by the better artist, and the change from the prose of *Morte Darthur* to the poetry of *The Faerie Queene* was a transubstantiation.

Beyond the variety of story, incident, and decoration, again, there is in *The Faerie Queene* a variety of matter of more than purely artistic interest, which required study in other places than the works of the poets, but which had to be turned to poetry if its inclusion were to be justified.   As in the passage of the Sixth Book referred to above, many kinds of interest were combined and

[1] Du Bellay, *Deff. et Ill.*, p. 72.

multiplied, and the intelligent reader was intended to perceive and appreciate them all. This was part of the business of the poet, and especially of the epic poet. ' Because the kinds of knowledge which must be treated when events are narrated are various, Ariosto often shows himself to be very well versed in many sciences—as regards the sky and the earth by his knowledge of the stars and of cosmography, and as regards politics and war by the judgment which he shows himself to possess in military art and in affairs according to the merits attributed to this one and that.' [1]   ' It is useful also to the writer to talk with practitioners of those arts of which he is about to treat, with physicians, for instance, about the health of the body and the quality and nature of the members, with wise men about consultations, with astrologers about the heavens, with cosmographers about the earth and the sea, about rivers and voyages, with naturalists about the origins of things and their generation, with mariners about the art of navigation, with captains about wars, dispositions and feats of arms, with knights about chargers and jousts, with princes about the ruling of peoples and of cities, and (to go no farther) with all those of whose arts it will be needful for him to write ; for all that is in nature being a proper subject for the poet, and not less that which the liberal and mechanical arts have in themselves, it would be too great a burden if he had to learn all that before he set himself to write. And so it will suffice to discourse with those who have made of such things their study and are well practised in them.' [2]

---

[1] Pigna, *I Romanzi*, p. 80. Cf. Ronsard, Second Preface to *La Franciade*, p. 20.

[2] Giraldi Cinthio, *Discorsi*, p. 193.

Spenser's unsettled life gave him some knowledge of arts and crafts, but much of his learning, and one may imagine the part he was most interested in, came from books. His friend Harvey, who held that ' it is not sufficient for poets, to be superficial humanists : but they must be exquisite artists, and curious universal schollers,' and admired Chaucer and Lidgate for their ' astronomie, philosophie, and other parts of profound or cunning art,' tells us that ' Mr. Spenser conceives the like pleasure in the fourth day of the first Weeke of Bartas, which he esteems as the proper profession of Urania.' ' The same Spenser, though not entirely unacquainted with the sphere and the astrolabe, is ashamed of his lack of skill in canons, tables, and instruments.'[1] Spenser may be thought to know as much astronomy as a poet need, but the confession is significant. Harvey himself was no useless friend for a man of such mind. A follower of Ramus, he shared the ideas of the newer school ; his general arguments would continue, rather than conflict with, the teaching of Mulcaster, and he was an omnivorous reader, a lover of

> All kynde of bookes, good, and badd,
> Sayntish and Divelish, that ar to be hadd.
> Owlde, and yunge,
> For matter and tunge,
> Wheresoever they dwell,
> In Heaven, or in Hell ;
> Machiavell, Aretine, and whome you will,
> That ar any renownid for extraordinary skill.[2]

The verse is naught, but the sentiment is that of a true man of the Renaissance, and though Harvey's advice might not always be sound, it would do Spenser no harm

---

[1] Marginalia in Dionysius Periegetes. For *artists* the modern may read *scientists*.   [2] Letterbook (Camden Society), p. 134.

to be rallied on his longing after an idealized past,[1] and
Harvey's information and guidance in reading would
undoubtedly be useful. Spenser's philosophy must be
studied separately, but his taste for both arts and science
must be noted, and the variety in kind as well as in language of his sources. Holinshed ' much advantaged '
him in the preparation of *Epithalamion Thamesis*,[2] and the
debt is visible in the recension of that poem in *The Faerie
Queene*. Plutarch, and the chroniclers from Geoffrey of
Monmouth to his contemporaries Holinshed and Camden, provided the matter of his historical disquisitions,
Castiglione helped in the descriptions of the ideal
courtier, and Pliny was a quarry for natural history more
exotic and marvellous than the observation of huntsman
and falconer could supply, but thereby none the less
valuable for imagery. The list of Spenser's authorities
would be more in place in a commented text than in a
history ; the important matter at the moment is that he
made all his reading serve his poetry, and read widely in
many subjects that his poetry might be the richer and
the more exact.

Imitation, in one sense, was a means of acquiring
literary skill, an aid to expression and to invention ; in
the other sense, it was the very foundation of art.
' Invention is nothing other than the fine temper of
an imagination conceiving ideas and forms of all things,
both heavenly and earthly, animate and inanimate,
which can be imagined, in order to represent, describe,
and imitate them afterwards : for just as it is the aim
of the orator to persuade, so that of the poet is to imitate,
invent, and represent things which are, which may be,
or which the ancients believed to be true.'[3]   In the

[1] *Ibid.*, p. 86.   [2] *Elizabethan Critical Essays*, I, p. 100.
[3] Ronsard, *Art Poétique*, p. 321.

serious English mind the function of the poet as citizen bulked very large. For Spenser, as for Sidney, the poet was not justified by artistic success only ; his ' speaking picture ' was invented and set forth ' with this end, to teach and delight.' [1] It is unnecessary to enlarge upon the prevalence of this well-known didactic motive : it covered the philosophical, scientific, and political matter introduced among the artistic and emotional interests of a poetry which was intended to appeal to the intellect as well as to the other faculties of its readers, and still more it emphasized the moral and spiritual content of poetry and its effect upon the life of the reader. The speaking picture had to have a meaning ; that the duty should have been interpreted so literally as to result in allegory was perhaps a failure of the critical imagination, but it was pressed on Spenser from many directions.

The more or less covert personal allusions in the poems provide a problem for the biographer, but to account for their presence is simple enough. The precedents and the critical notion drawn from them have already been dealt with, and in any case, where an author is a member of a social circle the *roman à clef* is bound to occur. Mediaeval romances almost certainly contain allusions recognizable at the courts for which they were written ; Sidney's *Arcadia* had a key, as had the French romances of the seventeenth century. The political allegory of *The Faerie Queene* was but an extension of the same process, addressed to the wider circle of the nation ; the moral allegory is a more profound thing, and even more common. It was of the allegorical pictures of Rubens that Hazlitt was reminded as he read *The Faerie Queene*, but Spenser's first published work was related

[1] Sidney, *Apology* ; *Elizabethan Critical Essays*, I, p. 158.

to a more naïve type of allegorical picture, the Emblem,
a type which remained popular into the next century.
In these translations from du Bellay and Petrarch the
pictures in speech are doubled with pictures in line, and
the apocalyptic convention which Spenser employed again
in *Visions of the Worlds Vanity* and *The Ruines of Time*
is but one form of the emblematic method. If these
poems are the *Dreames* which Spenser mentions in his
letters to Harvey, they should have appeared with illustrations as well as with an explanatory commentary by
E.K.[1] The picture exists in such case to impress on
the reader's mind the image formed by the poet, and
the image is symbolic of intellectual and moral or spiritual
values quite apart from its own æsthetic value. The
Emblem is the crudest example of Sidney's principle,
' a speaking picture, with this end, to teach and delight,'
that is, the crudest manifestation of Spenser's theory of
poetry.

The habit was, of course, an inheritance from the
Middle Ages. To the mediaeval mind the double meaning of things was ever present, for symbolism was the
only link between the material and the spiritual, still
more between the moral and the physical. A purely
metaphysical philosophy, seeking clarity and definition
by means of strict logic, could not embrace, and could
not allow itself to be affected by, æsthetic considerations,
the more that it was in close and permanent relations
with a theology which deliberately negated the material
and denounced the pleasures of the senses as leading to
damnation. Such a philosophy and such a theology
only condescended upon the material world when by a
purely intellectual process the physical manifestation could

---

[1] Postscript to second letter to Harvey.

be made to shadow a spiritual significance, and except where music, poetry, decoration, architecture were used to create religious (not æsthetic) emotion, the arts, including literature, secured themselves only by serving that end or by remaining frankly and completely profane, and in either case they tended to adopt the intellectual method of symbolism. That method ran through all thought and study and representation of material objects, as if trying to justify the existence of matter, from the semi-magical doctrine of sympathies, through the technical terms of alchemy, to the interpretation of the poets, and even of the florid music of the late fifteenth century. The arid dullness of a Berchorius, cataloguing the symbolic relationships of all things of earth with those of heaven, might be dismissed as a disease, were he not merely the deadliest pedant of a whole system according to which, as in the works of Aldovrandi, the emblematic significance of birds and beasts and trees was appended as a matter of course to scientific and literary observations. Early humanists made a stand against this vicious mechanism, as Colet did notably in upholding the literal interpretation of the Bible, but a habit is not so easily destroyed, and the importance of art was still conceived to lie, not in its æsthetic values, whose spiritual nature was not appreciated, but in the intellectual, moral, and theological values it could be made to symbolize.

The humanists may be given the credit of rediscovering pure æsthetic value, but even with them it was contaminated with the habit of allegory. Allegory justified the adoption of a pagan mythology, that very valuable and attractive mass of poetic material which the new learning made more available to the new poets than it had been to their elders. That poetic mythology had already undergone interpretation by commentators both early and late, and the reconstituted Pantheon was accepted as allegorical. ' The writer of romances has difficulty in making an invocation : for to call upon Our Lord or turn to the Saints in fabulous matters would be heresy rather than religion. To take refuge with Apollo and the chorus of the Muses would be improper, since such deities are accepted only among the Gentiles. But rather it will be useful to feign that some good spirit, by whom we are incited to poetry, is Apollo or the chorus of Muses, and the former and the latter are valuable to us not for vain superstition, but to denote that divine fury.'[1] Giraldi Cinthio forbids the introduction of the ancient Gods—unless the subject is ancient, when decorum permits it—and also of the Christian ; ' Whence, seeing this, the writers who have treated of Christian things invented by themselves, in order to avoid this impropriety, have introduced Fairies, and instead of ancient false and lying Gods (as Dante said) have made infernal spirits appear, and have feigned incantations, by means of which they have brought into their poems the same effects as the Greek and Latin poets did before by means of their Gods.'[2] This problem troubled the anxious soul of Tasso, but Spenser had no compunctions, for his mythology has a philosophical significance, or could be explained in the words of Ronsard : ' The Muses, Apollo, Mercury, Pallas, and other such deities represent to us nothing other than the powers of God, to Whom the first men gave several names for the divers effects of His incomprehensible Majesty.'[3] It would

---

[1] Pigna, *I Romanzi*, p. 82.   [2] Giraldi Cinthio, p. 69.

[3] Ronsard, *Art Poétique*, p. 319.

be idle to assert that the employment of the ancient mythology did not at times degenerate into frigid or listless formalism, and Ronsard's argument may be taken as a special plea against the charge of paganism, but the argument is there, and may be allowed. These were old names given to mysterious forces and powers ; their associations were delightful to a scholar-poet, and by virtue of their previous handling by masters of poetry they were tractable in verse.

With these symbols of the obscure workings of the life-forces of earth men had made beautiful and meaning-ful poetry ; and in the last resort man requires a mytho-logy for the expression of his profoundest and most exalted intuitions. A poet may make a mythology for himself, as did Blake, but no one will understand it but himself ; or he may adopt that which is the common possession of all educated men, the most beautiful and most complete, the mythology of Greece and Rome. Spenser handled that mythology freely, never hesitating to give his own turn to a story, a name, or an interpreta-tion, for the verse's sake or to suit his argument. He used it for what significance it held or he could put into it : these were poets' stories, and as a poet he could do as he pleased with them, to make them suitable for his own purposes. They were valuable because they did express forces, where the other mythology he inherited, the mediaeval mythology of the *Romance of the Rose*, only personified abstractions. The mediaeval figures are faint and powerless ; they have to be labelled with their names, Faux-Semblant, Bel-Accueil, Danger, and their actions can be understood only through their names. Spenser showed his appreciation both of their decorative quality and of their lifelessness by representing them only in picture or pageant, but he used them none the less, with the mediaeval picture of Cupid and his subjects which attracted Petrarch and Marot before him.

Not only mythology, however, but other elements of ancient poetry received an allegorical interpretation, as we have already seen. The moral significance of the epic, in particular, accepted as dogma by generations, was bound to lead to that. It could be traced back to Horace, in the second of his first book of Epistles, it may be found among critics of authority as late as Boileau, and in its turn Romance was commended by Giraldi Cinthio as superior even to Epic for this purpose. Spenser's letter to Raleigh testifies to his acceptance of the duty of moral teaching and to his belief in allegory as the means of its fulfilment ; in taking up the position of a moral allegorist he was not abdicating from that of romantic or epic poet. 'Proclus and other Platonists, and . . . Plutarch among the Peripatetics, defend Homer from the objections made against him, by no other defence than allegory.'[1] With this and similar arguments Tasso consoled himself for the allegory of his Christian romance-epic. His allegory was a painful afterthought, produced for the purpose of justifying his *Gerusalemme Liberata* to the Rome of the Counter-Reformation ; Spenser's was freely adopted for a chosen purpose of inculcating moral and spiritual truth. Spenser's difficulty, or perhaps rather his reader's, lies in his intermediate position, with the inherited habit of allegory strong in him and at the same time the Renaissance instinct of the value of the senses and of their cultivation in art. The intellectual activity did not supersede the æsthetic, or even coalesce with it so completely as, for instance, in Dante, and he

[1] *Lettere Poetiche,* 1587, p. 51 *vo.*

might say with Tasso : ' I do not believe it is necessary that the allegory should correspond in every particle to the natural meaning, since no such allegory is to be seen, not even those of Plato, which are the most exact. In Homer and Virgil the allegory is found only in certain Books. And Marsilio Ficino [in his commentary] on the *Symposium* quotes these words of St. Augustine : " Not all things which are feigned in figures are to be thought to have significance ; for many things are added, along with those that have significance, for the sake of order and connexion." '[1]

The confusion wrought by doubling moral and philosophical allegory with *roman à clef* and permitting literary and artistic interests to suspend or supersede both, is increased by the employment of different modes of allegory ; or, to put it more accurately, Spenser makes a heavy claim on his reader's intelligence by requiring him to be alive to all these interests together, and makes that claim the heavier by employing different modes of allegory. Much of the poetry he was brought up on, and brought up to imitate in both matter and manner, were allegorical in intention or, as has been noted, were apt to receive allegorical interpretation, and these were not uniform either in method or in purpose. The opposite poles are the symbolic personification after the manner of the *Romance of the Rose* (the mediaeval French convention inherited from Chaucer), and the true myth as

---

[1] *Ibid.* Tasso's *Discorsi e Lettere Poetiche* have not been quoted much in the present volume, because they appeared too late to have much effect on Spenser's ideas or on the planning of his poems. Though, however, Spenser could come by all his ideas without Tasso's critical work, it is of value as casting light on the point of view of the times, and it may have contributed *post factum*—to the Letter to Raleigh.

he saw it in Plato.   Between these lie the parable of the
preacher, the fable, the interpretation of mythology, the
exemplary episode, the simple but suggestive story, the
illustration of a truth or of a theory, the dramatic personification as distinct from the symbolic, and intermediate
modes not easy to define.   These various modes were not
selected according to a scheme, but instinctively as the
matter formed itself in the poet's mind, or of necessity
as he borrowed, nor are they easy to disentangle ; there
is personification in Virgil as well as in Chaucer, myth
in the *Romance of the Rose* as well as in the *Phaedrus*,
and parable in both the Bible and the *Symposium*.   Spenser probably never differentiated them clearly to himself, though he cannot but have been aware of the difference of his own approach to the various matter.   Sometimes he mingles one with another, sometimes passes
from one to another, awkwardly or easily yet always with
a certain security of instinct, and, in moral if not in
personal questions, with perfect lucidity.

The main conception of the various knights as pro-
tagonists of the various virtues is a natural procedure
which may be explained in several ways.   Personification is employed to give definition to an abstraction, a
generalization, any non-material entity ; the dramatic
value of a character may be made more obvious by simplification, until only the essential characteristic is left ;
stories tending to the same end, or displaying the same
characteristic, gather round a well-known or traditional
figure.   Spenser would be familiar with all these, in the
moralities and interludes, in the *Romance of the Rose*, in
fables and fabliaux, in the romances which made Lancelot the type of nobility and Gawaine of courtesy.   They
were all in his mind together, and his motive varies from

one to another. Normally, and originally, his persons
are personifications, but not necessarily or invariably :
the magician Archimago personifies Deceit, but the
magician Merlin is an historical character ; in the second
canto of Book III Britomart is simply a girl in love, in
the last she is Chastity in presence of the forms of Desire,
in the sixth canto of Book IV, a woman courted by a
man. Once the person is established, the exemplary
episode and the illustration follow, and these may be
symbolic, as the sojourn of Guyon in the House of Alma,[1]
or dramatic, as Arthegall's argument with the Giant,[2]
or parabolic, as where the Red Cross Knight and Una
lose their way in the Wood of Error,[3] or typical action
—what Minturno would call ' manners decorous with
the character '—as the episode (borrowed from Ariosto)
in which Britomart is insulted by the unchaste love of
Malecasta [4] ; or they may be mingled, as the story of
Malbecco and Hellenore changes from a fabliau into a
myth.[5] The subject and the origins of the different
Books naturally affect the method. Thus the Legend
of Holiness, which is principally biblical, tends towards
parable, that of Temperance, based on the Bible and
on Aristotle, towards myth, while that of Courtesy,
though its general scheme is symbolic, is worked out
mainly by a series of illustrations. But all methods
are employed in every Book, and every Book is diversified
and complicated with innumerable minor allegories and
myths invented for the purpose of the moment or borrowed from the poets, from moralists like Seneca and
Plutarch, from mythologists like Cicero and Macrobius

[1] II, ix.   [2] V, ii.
[3] I, i.   [4] III, i.
                    [5] III, x.

and commentators like Servius on Virgil and Landino
on Petrarch, and searched for, verified, or amplified
in Pliny and Aulus Gellius and Boccaccio and Nat-
alis Comes and all the philosophers ancient and
modern.

No principle is to be found, but the thing can be
explained. Three different forces are involved, the
intellectual, the æsthetic, and the humane. Where the
proposition appears first as an intellectual conception, it
may be expressed by means of parallelism, in a symbol
which represents without 'imitating' (as the Rose of Love,
the Christian armour, or in a parable), and the reader may
decipher the matter back into its original terms. The
true myth expresses a philosophic intuition for which
no terms exist ; by appealing through artistic feeling
to the imagination of the reader it goes farther than
intellect can, and so cannot be translated completely in
any other way. The illustration appeals directly to the
reader's common humanity through the simpler emotions. All these methods of enforcing a meaning were
familiar to Spenser, as has been said, and he used them
all because he needed them all. The parable can easily
be overdone, and it may even become an encumbrance
rather than a help ; the myth has this danger, that it
may be accepted too literally—it is not always possible
to tell in Plato what is myth and what serious philosophical argument ; the lesson of the exemplary or cautionary
tale is easily lost sight of. Spenser was trying to deal
with a great variety of matter, and to satisfy a great variety
of interests, and he tried every method he knew, from
the love-story of Britomart and Arthegall on one hand
and the symbolic pageantry of the Castle of Alma and the
House of Busyrane on the other, to the great vision of

the Gods in the Seventh Book and the philosophic myth of the Garden of Adonis, that his speaking picture might delight and teach, might convey to England the treasure of his thought and his learning.

CHAPTER VI

Philosophy

The basic fact of the Renaissance, so difficult to isolate, has been held to be the escape of human reason from the bonds of authority. It would be true also to say that it was the escape of human temperament from the bonds of reason, from the habit of categorical division which is the mark of the legalistic mind of the Middle Ages. The mediaeval man kept things separate, and attended to one at a time. The Griselda of the Clerk's Tale, for instance, offends a modern reader by her lack of proper pride ; the Clerk's Tale, however, is not about proper pride, but about patience. So also the passivity of Emily in the Knight's Tale is sometimes cited as a social document, evidence for the position of women in the Middle Ages, but the Knight's Tale is not about the relations of a young lady with two young men who are fighting over her, nor about her ideas or emotions, but about the relations of two friends who find themselves in enmity, and about the proper conduct of their quarrel. On the larger scale, the simple emotion of the *Acta Sanctorum* is divided from the austere logic of the *Summa Theologiæ* ; Guillaume de Lorris expounds a law that is neither Canon nor Civil, but chivalric ; the religious emotion of the story of the Saint Graal does not affect the ethics of the story of Tristram and Iseult in the same book. This separation of human functions and interests could not last for ever, and when it weakened there began the Renaissance, the discovery of man as a whole, indivisible, mind and body and soul together—the discovery of the central inclusive fact of Life. On one hand the evasion of temperament broke down the dominion of mediaeval intellectualism, leading philosophy away from metaphysics, which exercised only logic, to ethics, which implies the co-operation with intellect of intuition and feeling ; and on the other hand it removed ethics from the sole jurisdiction of dogmatic and inexpugnable ecclesiasticism, to be examined in the light of thought and experience. Men discovered that their own actions and emotions were really the most interesting subject in the world, and felt they were not receiving the serious attention they deserved. Scholastic philosophy ignored them, the Church pronounced judgment upon them, sometimes in accordance with an ascetic ideal too high for the ordinary mortal and sometimes in accordance with clerical aims which the world's honesty condemned, and the secular literature of chivalry dealt with them only in the limited sphere of social convention.

Love between man and woman, for example, could not be discussed by scholastic philosophers with any profit to lovers. The Church regarded sex as an evil —even if it were a necessary evil—and recognized its existence only by imposing restrictions on it. The chivalric poets treated of it without regard to ethics at all : Sir Gawaine's reason for refusing to commit adultery, for instance, is purely social—it would be discourteous to the husband, who is his host.[1] But this was one of the great human facts whose interest the

[1] *Gawaine and the Green Knight*, lines 1773–5.

Renaissance felt pressing, and it had to be considered in all its bearings. So also with Justice and Temperance and Glory, and all the other vital factors in man's existence ; they escaped the categories of truth and falsehood, of holiness and sinfulness, of good form and bad form, not because these categories did not apply, but because they all applied. Taken separately in the mediaeval manner, they were too narrow and too rigid, and so men turned to the classics, where the conditions of man's life and the factors of his destiny are treated under wider and more elastic terms of good and evil. In the classics, again, a less dogmatic theory of the state, the ideas of civic duty and of expediency, the political virtues and vices, were included among those conditions and factors, and the sense of beauty and its cultivation in art, disregarded by the Schoolmen and denounced by the Church, but very living in the eager temperament, permeated all the thought and expression of the ancients. Few of the humanists, perhaps, and few of their disciples, could have formulated what it was that satisfied them in Plato and Cicero and Virgil, but the instinct, however obscure, was powerful, and when the new poets set themselves to school to the classics it was to acquire not only the finer art, but this wider scope, this adequacy to life as a whole, which even the best of the vernacular poets had missed. The humanists led them to Lucretius, the poet who was a philosopher, and to Plato, the philosopher who was a poet, and they, proposing to themselves the creation of a philosophic poetry, a poetry which should treat of human life in all its aspects and under all the categories of judgment, sought wisdom from the philosophers just as they sought guidance in their art from the critics.

One of the purposes of the new poetry was to bring into circulation among the modern peoples the treasures of the world's thought, for the sake of whatever use the peoples might make of them. The ideas of the philosophers formed part of Spenser's academic training, and part of the *materies* which it was his duty to treat in his dissimilar English manner. He incorporates into his own poems, accordingly, fragments from philosophic as well as from other writers, and for the same variety of reasons. When, for instance, he insets into his somewhat mediaeval description of the Court of Venus the first thirty-odd lines of the *de Rerum Natura* of Lucretius,[1] the passage has no special Epicurean significance ; the procedure is purely literary. In this Book Spenser was treating largely of Love. For the complete presentation of his theme he had been studying Lucretius, and when his poetic precedents called for a hymn to Venus, he imitated this excellent one. Here the literary motive is clear enough, but less purely artistic imitations cause endless doubt and difficulty, which can be overcome only by tactful consideration by the reader of each example as it occurs. A fragment of Aristotle or Seneca or Plato may be borrowed, not only for its beauty, but because it expressed more or less clearly some feeling which Spenser was trying to make explicit, and it may be borrowed just as a phrase or a story might be borrowed from Virgil or Ariosto. The use of quotations may be proof of study, but is not necessarily proof of intellectual discipleship, still less of complete acceptance of a system of thought. Nor did quotations necessarily come direct from their originals, for many phrases and arguments had done duty many times,

[1] Book IV, x, 44–7.

and not always the same duty or in the same connexion.

By an ordinary process, again—and we have seen Spenser bear his part in it—technical expressions, divorced from their original bearing, pass into the common stock of allusion, and thence, losing precision of reference and meaning by the way, into the common stock of current speech. It is one of the difficulties that confront the student of the Renaissance that the process was then both rapid and voluminous. Many common words and phrases, now almost empty of content, may at any occurrence in Renaissance work be understood as having their original connotation, or their modern, or anything between, and this is particularly noticeable in the work of Spenser, who kept a loose grip on language, and is apt, moreover, to use the technical terms of philosophy just as he uses those of law or of falconry, but with scarcely the same precision. In such a passage as the following, for instance, the term ' Idea ' is explicitly the technical term of Platonism :

> Faire is the heaven . . .
> More faire is that, where those Idees on hie
> Enraunged be, which Plato so admired.[1]

When in the *Hymne of Heavenly Love* the poet speaks of ' th' Idee ' of God's ' pure glorie,'[2] the difficulty of the conception may be caused by loose thinking—he means, presumably, the divine glory as seen in itself, not in an earthly reflection. In two of the *Amoretti*, however, the term appears to mean an image or representation in the mind :

---

[1] *Hymne of Heavenly Beautie*, 78–83.
[2] *Hymne of Heavenly Love*, 284.

Within my hart, though hardly it can shew
thing so divine to vew of earthly eye,
the fayre Idea of your celestial hew
and every part remaines immortally.[1]

Ne ought I see, though in the clearest day,
when others gaze upon theyr shadows vayne :
but th' onely image of that heavenly ray
whereof some glance doth in mine eie remayne,
of which beholding the Idaea playne
through contemplation of my purest part
with light thereof I feed my love-affamisht hart.[2]

These have been taken as a confession of Platonic faith, the record of progress from desire of beauty seen in the flesh to desire of beauty conceived in the intellect. The first, however, is a well-known commonplace, used by Marot[3] and derived from Serafino da Aquila. The second is closely related not only to Sonnet xxxv, but to Petrarch's Sonnet lxxi and Canzone xii, and still more to one of Bembo's *Rime* :

Mentre 'l fero destin me toglie, et vieta
Veder Madonna, e tiemmi in altra parte
La bella immagin sua veduta in parte
Il digiun pasce, e i miei sospiri acqueta.[4]

The Platonic source of Spenser's phrasing is obvious —he might not, perhaps, have disclaimed a Platonic sub-intention—but the use of the term 'idea' to mean 'image' can be paralleled in Ronsard[5] and Montaigne,[6]

---

[1] *Amoretti*, xlv.   [2] *Amoretti*, lxxxviii.
[3] Elegie xvi, 72–99.
[4] Ed. of 1548, fol. 31 *vo*. 'While cruel fate seizes me and forbids me to see my Lady, and keeps me in another place, her fair image seen in part feeds my hunger and quiets my sighs.'
[5] See quotation on p. 139.   [6] II, vi : *Of Exercise*.

and the employment of philosophical tags in many of
Ronsard's sonnets, as here :

> O lumière enrichie
> D'un feu divin qui m'ard si vivement
> Pour me donner et force et mouvement
> Estes-vous pas ma seule Entelechie ?[1]

which is not an Aristotelian psalm, but a compliment
to his lady's eyes. If, finally, Spenser intended the
full Platonic significance to be attached to these sonnets,
then he was a bad or at least a reluctant Platonist, for
surely the philosopher should rejoice at his achievement
of a step nearer the One, and here Spenser mourns.

It is not safe to argue Spenser's adherence to a system
of philosophy upon such uncertain evidence, and as for
more extensive borrowings, let the warning of three quotations suffice. ' It is easie to verifie,' says Montaigne,
' that excellent authors, writing of causes, do not only
make use of those which they imagine true, but eftsoones
of such as themselves believe not : always provided they
have some invention and beautie. They speake sufficiently, truly and profitably, if they speake ingeniously.
We cannot assure ourselves of the chiefe cause : we
hudle up a many together, to see whether by chance it
shall be found in that number.'[2] According to Ronsard,
as we have seen, the aim of the poet is ' to imitate, invent,
and represent the things which are, or can be, or which
the Ancients believed to be true.'[3] And after discussing
the variety of knowledge required by Ariosto for his
heroic poem, Pigna continues : ' And since in such
variety of different professions there may be opinions

---

[1] *Amours*, I, lxviii.   [2] III, vi : *Of Coaches* : tr. Florio.
[3] *Art Poétique*, p. 321.

of many philosophers, with which he comes in contact, he is here a Stoic, there a Platonist, and on one hand one opinion is followed, on another, another.'[1] Literary imitation and the careful exhibition of wide scholarship might almost be supposed to account for the appearance in Spenser's work of philosophic matter, were it not that deep thought was required of the new school of poetry, and that one of his purposes in *The Faerie Queene*, and that not the least important, was ' to fashion a gentleman or noble person in vertuous and gentle discipline.'   Holding such a purpose, he did not attempt to construct an original independent theory of morality. He lived in days before it was necessary to gain a reputation as moralist by showing that unchastity is chastity or that purity of soul is best manifested in a Russian debauch.   True to his classical training and to the profound common sense of his English character, trying to arrive at the central truth, the essential common factor which all men must recognize, he attempted rather an exposition of the general consensus of the best ethical doctrine.   Such a purpose required all the course of philosophic reading on which his Cambridge studies entered him, as well as his native and inherited instincts.

The method of *The Faerie Queene* is, to display each virtue completely in all its forms and phases, not as a simple characteristic, but as defined by the various trials and experiences operating to its perfection, by the various actions proper to its possession, and, negatively, by the diverse vices and defects opposed to it.   A single exemplar is not enough.   Guyon and the Palmer present Temperance arising from two different moral bases,

[1] *I Romanzi*, p. 81.

highmindedness and restraint ; Britomart and Belphœbe and Amoret, different conceptions of chastity—that which depends on strength and faithfulness, that which is a noble fastidiousness removed from common frailty, and that which is a natural attribute of womanly character. Spenser drives home his lesson by repeated variations, adding additional illustrations by additional characters and episodes. Sir Calidore, to take the simplest instance, represents Courtesy : his principal task is to restrain malice and evil speaking—the ' Male-Bouche ' of the chivalric allegorists—he also teaches mercy and mildness, championship of woman, tenderness to the sick, politeness to honest inferiors.[1] Cruelty, haughtiness, inhospitality, treachery, insincerity, are his opposites, though not necessarily his personal opponents in the story.[2] Tristram and the Hermit show that Courtesy, though rightly ' named of court,' belongs to ' the gentle blood ' and not to worldly position ; the Savage Man, that goodwill and right instinct are its primary conditions. Incidental illustrations are given in the old knight Aldus, who tempered his grief for his son's wounds

> and turned it to cheare
> To cheare his guests, whom he had stayed that night
> And make their welcome to them well appeare,[3]

and in the quaint worldly-wise diplomacy of Calidore's explanation of the lady Priscilla's absence from home.[4] Courtesy, again, is allied to Justice in Prince Arthur's punishment of Turpine,[5] its place in the sphere of Love

[1] Book VI, i, 40 ff. ; ii, 14 ; ii, 47–8 ; ix, 6–7, 18.
[2] Crudor, Briana, Maleffort, Turpine, Blandina.
[3] Canto iii, 6.   [4] Canto iii, 12–19.   [5] Canto vi, 18–vii, 27.

illustrated by the episode of Mirabella,[1] its interpretation extended by the vision of the Graces and Colin Clout's explanation.[2] Nor does this very rapid analysis by any means exhaust the complexity of Spenser's conception, which appears often in a phrase or even a pregnant word.

To frame and exhibit this complex conception of the virtues, then, required more than the current body of conventional social habit, and so Spenser draws upon the philosophers. The Sixth Book, as might be expected, contains least matter from classical sources : there are evident reminiscences of Seneca in many places,[3] but Chaucer and the romancers,[4] and the example of the best contemporaries, were authorities enough for Courtesy. Books which deal with more difficult questions, and questions which have been treated of by many minds, display a greater variety of sources, and Spenser evidently made a special study of the main authorities for each Book. It is only in the Sixth Book that Senecan borrowings appear in any quantity ; the Stoic doctrine of the right of suicide, for instance, is mentioned only to be condemned by the Red Cross Knight.

The Bible contributes much matter and phrase to the First Book, as well as the methods already noticed, because it is the authority for Holiness, as Aristotle is for Temperance and for Justice ; but ' in the multitude of professions ' other authorities are quoted, and the complete ethical conception—for be it noted that even Holiness

---

[1] Canto vii, 27–viii, 30.

[2] Canto x, 21–24.

[3] Cf. i, 12, 5–6 and Seneca, Ep. xxxv; vi, 6 ff., and Ep. viii, l, lxviii; vi, 14, and Ep. ix, xxv, lxiii ; ix, 20 ff., and Ep. ii, iv ; etc.

[4] Alluded to, iii, l. Cf. Wife of Bath's Tale, 257–60 ; *Rose*, 2196–7 *et passim.*

is an ethical conception, with only the slightest mystical infusion in the last canto—the complete conception is built up of many fragments drawn from many sources. The Books of Chastity and Friendship, which really deal with Love, are drawn from Lucretius as well as from the Nicomachean Ethics : that Spenser follows Aristotle generally in the Book of Justice by no means precludes his following Boethius or Plato, the Hebrew prophets, the institutes of chivalry, or the police system of contemporary Ireland, in any one passage. Some of Spenser's debts to the philosophers have been studied, and there is matter enough for more, but unfortunately none of these separate studies, though valuable in themselves, can give a proper idea of Spenser's philosophy, for the character of his thought, here as elsewhere, can be appreciated better through a rough grasp of his peculiar mixture of sources than by a complete study of one.

The difficulty—and the interest—arises from his equal acceptance of all available authorities ·: it should not be increased by over-simplification, by trying to confine Spenser to a school. He could accept all the ancient schools, all ' that the Ancients believed to be true,' just because they were all equally superseded by revealed religion. The fundamental fact about his ethics is that they were those of a Christian, a Protestant Christian with a tendency—not an indulged tendency —towards Calvinism. Like all the modern world, he inherited much ancient philosophy in the tradition of the Church and of society, which made easier the interfusion of one with another, but where he deliberately seeks the aid of the Schools it is as supplementary to the teaching of the Church of England, and borrowings

should be read only for their value at the moment and
not as committing Spenser to an alien, still less to a
pagan system.   He draws upon Seneca, and at the same
time upon the Epistle of St. James, upon Aristotle, and
upon the Apocrypha, the Prophets, the Book of Job,
the Revelation of St. John.   All are intimately mingled
together, but the Bible of all books was his principal
source, as it was the foundation of his faith.

This attempt to combine the best of all the philosophies within a predominant Christianity, the intimacy
with which the various borrowings are mingled, and the
occasional confusion which results, are typical of the time,
not only of the poets, but also of professed philosophers.
The men of the Renaissance, unlike those of the French
Revolution, were not seeking for a simplification ; they
had, as we have seen, just escaped from one, and they
rejoiced in the variety and complexity of life, of human
activities and possibilities, of human thought. They
were somewhat bewildered and confused by that variety,
those possibilities, but they faced them. There was
no one dominant or leading philosophy as there was
in the thirteenth century or even in the nineteenth, and
no system could be evolved until the intellectual excitement had calmed : only Calvin succeeded in working
out a complete system, and his system, confined to the
sphere of theology, excludes many considerations very
important to the average thinker of the time. Calvin
succeeded because he worked by pure logic, but in this
he was alone in his time : his contemporaries could not
keep their temperament out of their thinking, and their
doctrines, and the choice of authority to support them,
are not the result of severe process. Thinking to them
was an art and an indulgence, and it is by strength of

temperament rather than by novelty of thought, that that passionate thinker Giordano Bruno is the typical Renaissance philosopher. Bruno has been held to have influenced Spenser, but they worked towards different ends, Bruno in ardent speculation, Spenser in solid ethics. The phrases of Bruno may appear in Spenser, but the ideas they hold in common are not those peculiar to Bruno, but those which they could both find in Lucretius and Plato, and even the phrases are uncertain, for both phrase and idea were of the common stock of the time. The curious mixture of schools, and the loose handling and uncertain application of terms and formulas taken from various and often from conflicting sources, resulted from the attempt to gather and reconcile all the philosophies and to relate the mass to Christianity. It is the same process, though in the wider sphere and with much less security in outcome, as we have seen in the critical thought of the new poets, and it is to be found in such popular philosophical works as that of Leone Hebreo, and in commentaries like that of Loys le Roy on the Symposium, work which may be only of historical interest, but must not therefore be neglected.

All these men were strongly affected by Platonism, for the reconciliation of ancient philosophies with Christian doctrine began with the Platonic Academy of Florence. Why Platonism was so attractive to the Renaissance mind is sufficiently clear from what has gone before—in Plato's works temperament and intellect move in harmony, humane feeling and exalted speculation, ethics and the spiritual universals, somehow interpenetrate and are fused into one. There was some common ground in the unrecognized Platonic element in the tradition of the Church, and still more community

in the temper of thought, for Plato was not only the
philosopher who taught, like the Church, that earth is
but the shadow of heaven, but the philosopher of Love
and Beauty and Desire, the poet-philosopher of the
beautiful, spiritual tales. Platonism, then, was cultivated, compressed, and spread abroad. The treatises
of Ficino, Politian, Pico della Mirandola—especially
his commentary on the Platonic *canzone* of Benevieni—
passed the tenets of the Florentine school into the mind
of all Europe. To put it bluntly, Platonism was the
fashion. It marched well with Petrarchism, it certainly
was inspiring, and it could be romanced about. There
would be room for surprise if Spenser had not caught
this fashion along with all the others of his time : where
he found the material for the *Hymnes in Honor of Love
and Beauty* is more difficult. He certainly knew some
of Plato's works at first hand, and used them, but the
systematic method of the *Hymnes* is of the Renaissance.
Ficino, the master of all Renaissance Platonists, would
be his master also, but the phrase of Lucretius,

Mother of love and of all worlds delight [1]

was already brought into Platonic exposition by Loys le
Roy [2] ; Bruno's *degli Heroici Furori* may have supplied
some of the matter, and so may Bembo's *Asolani*, and
Castiglione's *Corteggiano* (newly translated by Sir Thomas
Hoby), and Leone Hebreo, and Pico, and Benevieni.
It is more likely that Spenser knew all these than that he
did not : in any one of them he would find all or nearly
all he required for the *Hymnes*, and his slight uncertain-
ties of thought are probably due to this, that he was

---

[1] *Hymne in Honor of Beautie*, 16.
[2] 1559. Du Bellay translated the verse quotations for him.

versifying the common floating conception—though
not far from his books—rather than one hammered out
in his mind.

In Italy the Church had to restrain the growing cult
of systematized Neo-Platonism, for though the intention
was to reconcile it with Christian dogma, the Platonism
tended to swallow up the Christianity. In France and
England Neo-Platonism did not antagonize the Churches,
for the Reformation had preceded its introduction, and
the fact of open conflict upon well-defined grounds
forced men to take a side for one Church or another
and attached them the more passionately to the central
tenets of their creed. The infusion of Platonism into
the thought of Christian men could do no harm, for
there was no possibility of competition and no possible
place for paganism. In the dedicatory epistles prefixed
to the *Fowre Hymnes* Spenser apologizes for those in
honour of Love and Beauty as having been written ' in
the greener times of my youth,' and in the *Hymnes* of
Heavenly Love and Heavenly Beauty he attempts to
sanctify his old Neo-Platonism by treating the Neo-
Platonic scheme as a myth, to symbolize the progress of
the Christian soul. The attempt, though productive
of some beautiful phrases, is neither very lucid philosophy
nor very downright theology ; it required more logic
than Spenser cared to spend in a poem ; but it shows
that the Platonic fashion ceased to prevail with a man
isolated from fashion and deeply engaged in the war of
the Churches. Platonism attracted him, always, as it
attracted many of his contemporaries, more as an emotion
than as a creed—in which he was perhaps the nearer Plato.

For the purposes of *The Faerie Queene* the Neo-
Platonists were less useful than the practical teachers

of ethics like Aristotle and Seneca : which means, of course, that Spenser was less interested in the Neo-Platonists. When Castiglione wrote his treatise *Il Corteggiano*, he, like Spenser, intended it 'to fashion a gentleman or noble person in vertuous and gentle discipline,' and when he broached the inevitable problem of the relation of the sexes he put into the mouth of Bembo, as the author of the *Asolani*, a brief resumé of Platonic doctrine, telling how the lover progresses from desire of beauty in one human embodiment to desire of that beauty divorced from flesh, so to desire of universal beauty, and so to God, Who is Beauty Itself. Now this is just what Spenser did not do in the poem into which he poured all he knew and felt and learned about the good life. In view of a common tendency among writers on this subject it is necessary to premise that to derive from Plato any and every conception of love higher than the brute instinct is a libel on mankind. There have been honourable souls in other states than Athens, and one element in the Platonic temperament, the yearning mood, the vague desire for far-away or half-imagined beauty, is common to all youth and to many peoples—to Kormak the Icelander, and Jaufré Rudel, and many an old poet of Germany and Ireland. ' Platonic Love ' as a deliberately accepted and conclusive ethic flourished in Italy, and, with Maurice Scève, in the Italianate city of Lyons : it may be doubted whether it suited the solid mind of the North, except as a scholarly elegance. The exaltation of beauty into something divine flattered the Renaissance temperament—almost gave an excuse for indulgence—and the spiritualization of love was easily grafted on the tradition of *amour courtois* to make a courtly refinement. But that very tradition carried a principle hostile to the Neo-Platonic scheme. Under Renaissance Neo-Platonism the only duty of woman is to be beautiful, to awaken desire, and then to disappear, leaving the desire to be nursed into an ecstasy in which she has no place : this cannot be reconciled with the principle of personal loyalty, the first clause of the law of *amour courtois* as it was the basis of the whole mediaeval system. And behind the principle of personal loyalty lies the secular instinct of the North, obvious enough for a stranger like Tacitus to have observed it, giving the woman her equal share in a love which exists for both man and woman together, and exists by virtue of their being man and woman.

Plato contributed largely to Spenser's thought, but he was not the only source of principle, nor was he the final authority. He enforced the truth that love is a spiritual activity, but the complementary truth that love is a primary function of the animate universe, essential to its continuance, was set forth with equal force by Lucretius, and these two principles were reconciled for Spenser in the final authority, the teaching of the Church of England, defined in the Marriage Service of the Prayer Book. Heavenly Love and Earthly are not eternal antagonists, but complements one of the other, and so the story of Chastity is a love-story. All Spenser's virtues are positive fighting virtues, and Chastity among them : its representative is neither nun nor sage, but a redoubtable knight who is also a woman in love, destined to the honourable estate of matrimony and the procreation of a noble line ; for chastity is nothing other than truth and honour in the question of sex, sanctified by the spirit of God, Who is Love, and serving the world as His agent. Chastity is attended by Prudence, but depends on its own strength and courage. It is as free from the asceticism of the Middle Ages and the asceticism of the Neo-Platonists as it is from the frauds and counterfeits, the weaknesses and the perversions it combats, for its end is not in the solitary individual soul, but in the universe, through love, of which it is the necessary condition.

This is the mark of Spenser's Puritanism. His removal from Cambridge took him out of the ecclesiastical controversies about vestments and altar-tables into a wider sphere of thought, but the essential of Puritanism remained with him, the sense of personal responsibility which cannot be transferred to priest or king. In his preaching of this doctrine he was, perhaps, as well in the example of his art, the master of Milton, who in a famous passage of *Areopagitica* dared think him 'a better teacher than Scotus or Aquinas.' False Puritanism is distinguished by its negations, but the true Puritan is not an ascetic, undergoing privations as a sacrifice or in self-distrust, but an athlete and a soldier, disciplining himself against indulgences which would unfit him here and now for his duty, and for the reward to be earned, not by the privations, but by the duty accomplished. The individual is responsible for himself, for his own destiny, and for more than his own : he is a combatant in the eternal strife between good and evil for the dominion of a universe in which spiritual and material are one. His victories and his defeats affect the universe as a whole, and he is never fighting alone. Ethics, then, takes a large place in Puritan thought, as the rule of a daily life which is an activity of the universe.

Individual human conduct, though perhaps concerned

in any one instance with small material conditions, extends into the great movement which is ultimately spiritual, just as the individual human life is part of the universal. In his study of love as the law of life Spenser extends ethics into speculation, for in it there is some hint of a solution to the problem which recurs through all his work, the problem of change. The mutability of things, the brevity of life, the inevitable end of human beauty and greatness, haunted the Renaissance as it haunted the Middle Ages ; but unlike the mediaeval poets Spenser was not content to accept it only as tragedy or as a subject for moralizing, for the problem was enlarged, made more poetic in being made more philosophical, by Lucretius. On this note *The Faerie Queene*, as we have it, closes, and we do not know how Spenser proposed to treat the Legend of Constancy, but it is in all his thought. His astronomical knowledge, however incomplete, destroyed for him even the poetic fiction of the changeless stars [1] : all earth was involved in change. That he learned to accept as a universal law : substance is constant, form changes according to universal law ; and Universal Law is God.

> What wrong then is it, if that when they die,
> They turne to that, whereof they first were made ?
> All in the powre of their great Maker lie :
> All creatures must obey the voice of the most hie. [2]

That is the theological statement, in a passage based on the second chapter of the first Book of Samuel and on Lucretius : it is stated again in the sixth canto of the Third Book, in the famous myth of the Garden of Adonis,

[1] Introduction to Book V ; VII, vii, 49–55.
[2] V, ii, 40.

12

compiled from the *Phaedrus*, the *Tabula* ascribed to
Cebes, Aristotle *de Anima*, Lucretius, and the Book of
Genesis.   Here the principle of continuance in change
is the Venus of Lucretius, presiding over procreation,
and representing ' nothing other than the power of God.'
Thus Love is doubly sanctified, matter and spirit are
reconciled, and the tragedy of mutability is resolved,
not by blind submission or by abstention, but by com-
prehension.

That is one solution of the problem of change : form
begets form in perpetuity according to the will of the
Creator ; but man cannot forget that which was, and in a
universe of unceasing change his desire is for stability.
In the last resort the only permanence is with God :

> When I bethinke me on that speech whyleare
> Of Mutabilitie, and well it way,
> Me seemes that though she all unworthy were
> Of the Heav'ns Rule, yet very sooth to say,
> In all things else she beares the greatest sway :
> Which makes me loath this state of life so tickle,
> And love of things so vaine to cast away
> Whose flowring pride, so fading and so fickle,
> Short Time shall soon cut down with his consuming sickle.

> Then gin I thinke on that which Nature sayd,
> Of that same time when no more change shall be,
> But stedfast rest of all things, firmely stayd
> Upon the pillours of Eternity,
> That is contrayr to Mutabilitie ;
> For all that moveth doth in Change delight :
> But thence-forth all shall rest eternally
> With Him that is the God of Sabaoth hight :
> O! that great Sabaoth God, grant me that Sabaoths sight.[1]

---

[1] VII, viii—the last fragment of *The Faerie Queene*.

But the positive spirit of England, of the time and the man, would not allow Spenser to wait in mystical contemplation for the coming of the Kingdom of Heaven. In this world of change men must strive for such stability as may be won by the strength of their virtues, and so the ethical ideal returns with renewed importance and validity. Yet Puritanism did not make Spenser a rebel. Just as the individual must be a well-disposed member of the universal life, so he must be a well-disposed citizen, for the state and the universe are maintained by order and control. The lesson of *The Faerie Queene* is the same throughout : society must be held together by concord or Friendship, the individual must be controlled by Temperance, the state by Justice. The recurrent victory of the trained and disciplined knights over ' the rascal many ' was more than an inheritance from the aristocratic Middle. Ages, or an echo of Tudor statesmanship, or a memory of Irish insurrections. All these were in Spenser's mind, but they were contained within the greater idea, the necessity of stability. The rabble is crushed because it is a rabble, incapable of constant policy of united action.

Spenser's political attitude is thus similar to that of Shakespeare, and for good cause. As *Paradise Lost* proclaims the individualism of the seventeenth century, so *The Faerie Queene* sums up the lesson of English history for a century and a half. There was reason in the adulation of Queen Elizabeth : she stood for the sixteenth-century virtues as Queen Victoria for those of the late nineteenth, and she had given England something approaching civil and religious stability for over thirty years when the first part of *The Faerie Queene* was published. In English history Shakespeare saw the

clash of personality and the permanence of England :
Spenser, less interested in the dramatic personality than
in the idea of movement, saw the eternal vicissitude of
things exemplified, and the need for stability enforced.
Partly this may be the reflection of the official mind,
largely it is the conclusion of the philosophical temper.
The great vision of Spenser is the vision of Mutability,
the alteration of the stars in their courses, the succession
of the months and seasons and centuries, the cycle of
birth and death, the sequence of kings and dynasties,
all subject to the universal law.

> For all that lives, is subject to that law :
> All things decay in time, and to their end do draw.[1]

Yet there is the permanent factor :

> That substance is eterne, and bideth so,
> Ne when life the decayes, and forme does fade,
> Doth it consume, and into nothing go,
> But chaunged is, and often altred to and fro.
>
> The substance is not chaunged, nor altered,
> But th' only forme and outward fashion.[2]

So in every particle of existence, in man, in society, in
the state, the temporary form is important as a phase of
the permanent, and must therefore be brought to its
best mode and noblest function.

Here, then, is justified the cultivation of all the activities of human life which was the contribution of the
Renaissance to the progress of the world. Spenser
could not set aside the material for the sake of the spiritual,

[1] III, vi, 40.
[2] III, vi, 37-38.

nor could he live in the material in despite of God. All
knowledge, art, beauty, emotion, government, manners,
were important as promoting the fine fashioning of the
universal substance, and as fashioning it towards permanence, for permanence is possible only in perfection.
We do not know what were the twelve virtues which
together made up Magnificence, but they were not
merely theological virtues. The six we have are Holiness, a spiritual virtue ; Temperance and Chastity,
personal virtues ; Justice, a political virtue ; Friendship
and Courtesy, social virtues ; and all these are shown
to be intimately interrelated and equally required of the
inclusive virtue of Magnificence. This complete and
balanced cultivation of all the powers of man was the ideal
of the Renaissance : Sidney displayed it in his life,
Shakespeare dramatically, Spenser philosophically. The
great man must be competent in each function, must
possess the capacity for thought, the capacity for feeling,
and the capacity for action, all trained and cultivated, and
all in equilibrium. Hamlet, Lear, Othello are subjects
of tragedy because one of their capacities is overbalanced,
though it may be only for the time, by the others : Spenser's ideal knights are victorious, because they are in
possession and in control of all three. The only permanence is in perfection—that is, in God—but something may be done on earth by the careful maintenance
of equilibrium. Thus Temperance is the personal
ideal which gives its due place to all the faculties of mind
and body by refusing dominion to any one, Justice the
political ideal which gives its due rights to each unit of
the state, prescribes to each its duties and keeps each
within its rights and its duties, Courtesy the social ideal
which gives each man his due of proper regard in

his degree and restrains the overbearing and the un-
gracious.

How much of this Spenser learned from Aristotle is
very obvious, as his debt to Plato is obvious, but as we
have seen, he was thirled to neither of them. The
attempts that have been made to discover the source of
the Twelve Virtues in Aristotle or in his commentators
have all been unsuccessful, and it would be more surprising to find than to miss it. Some credit must be
given to Spenser : just as the new poets combated the
notion that all the world's store of poetic power has been
expended on the earlier races, so they would have claimed
for the modern age some power of thought, if only because Christianity had reoriented many of the ancient
problems. There were to be twelve Books in *The
Faerie Queene* because that was the correct number for
an epic poem, not because there were any twelve virtues ;
and the phrase of Spenser ' the twelve private morall
vertues, as Aristotle hath devised,' is best and most
simply understood to mean ' the twelve moral virtues
which are such as Aristotle would call *private* virtues.'
Artistic motives must be kept in mind as well as philosophic, and temperament as well as reason. Thus Plato
appealed to the spiritual and artistic nature of the poet,
and Lucretius to his feeling for this world that is caught
in the whirl of change—and, since temperament must
judge of temperament, one reader at least feels that the
deeper communion of spirit was between Spenser and
Lucretius, that there is a depth of tone in the Lucretian
passages of *The Faerie Queene* more moving and more
heartfelt than the somewhat shrill straining of the *Hymnes*
of Love and Beauty. But if one name be asked for, as
of him who most formed the thought, and the habit of

thought, of Spenser, then it were best, here also, to turn
back to his early training, and there, of all thinkers that
he would be made to study, we find the prose idol of the
humanists, Cicero. *The Faerie Queene*, with much in
it *de Natura Deorum*, is the *de Officiis* and the *de Finibus*
of the Renaissance, deriving the elements of a complex
civic and personal ideal from the opinions of many philosophers, aiming at stability and the proper distribution
of rights and duties in an uncertain world, with a back-
ward glance at the pristine virtues of the past and yet a
wide outlook on the universe, preaching the search for
' what order may be, what it may be that is seemly and
fitting, a measure in speech and action,' observing man's
relations with God, with his fellows, and with the state.

Spenser was not a mere critic of life, but a constructive
idealist, and intent on a possible ideal. All his virtues,
as has been said, are positive fighting virtues, and go to
build up the positive ideal of Magnificence, magnani-
mity. Magnificence seems vague and uncertain. The
place of Prince Arthur in the epic-romance was never
quite clearly worked out ; his appearances are fitful and
unrelated, and this naturally obscures the expression of
the virtue he represents, but we know that Magnificence
includes all the others, and its difficulty is due to its
complexity. The Renaissance would forgo nothing and
would shirk nothing, but endeavoured to combine in
one comprehensive plan of life all personal and political
good, religion, learning, and all arts and elegances. It
is the most complex ideal that any poet ever attempted to
express, inclusive of all that Virgil ceded to Greece and
all he claimed for Rome, all the gifts and graces of
Chaucer's knight and squire and clerk and parson, and
all the art of Virgil and Chaucer with them. Intellect

and feeling had to combine in it, and to combine equally. Spenser's philosophy lacked the lucidity and system of severe intellectual process, but at least it did not attain lucidity and system by a severe process of exclusion of all that might interfere with its security. And among all our philosophic poets that may be said of Spenser alone.

CHAPTER VII

'*The Prince of Poets in his Tyme*'

The meaning of the term ' art ' may be narrowed down
as much as one pleases, but before the critic can define
the quality of the art of an individual, and after he has
isolated it, the historian must study the wider term
' work.' The artist's own conception of his art, and his
relation, and the relation of his work, to other art and
to life in general, must be considered. For the artist,
far from being a mere particle of æsthetic potentiality,
is a man like other men, a citizen and a moral being, with
a man's complexity of desires and interests. His peculiar means and methods of working depend upon his
intense æsthetic perception and his instinct to organize
his perceptions into creation, but all the time he expresses
his inner sense of the values of things, and that is developed and maintained by other activities of intellect
and feeling besides the æsthetic. Moral, philosophical,
religious, social, political opinions are as much a part of
his world as any other man's, and it is a false simplification to deny or minimize them, and a false delicacy
to deplore their appearance in his work. If this is not
so, then all the great poets have conceived wrongly of
their own business, and especially the great Renaissance
poets, and Spenser, as the latest and most typical of
them, most of all. Such men would, one imagines,
have considerable difficulty in understanding some

modern controversies about art and the artist, and might resent attempts to deprive them of intellectual, moral, social and civil rights and responsibilities. Both ' art for art's sake ' and ' art for life's sake ' would mean little to men who believed in art as a noble and necessary part of the complete and well-ordered life, and in their own work as their contribution to the full and various activity of the universe. The ideal Spenser taught was one of strenuous effort towards the perfection of that full and various activity, and he like other men had his manifold duty of service to the state, to his country, to man, and to God. It was his misfortune that his business as poet and his business as administrator in an uncongenial district marched together so badly, but if at times he longed for personal security and learned retirement, it was that he might the more fully cultivate his own gift, by which he might contribute the more to the general good in his own way.

The task he assumed in professing poetry was quite enough to absorb all his working life ; his resentment at the partial failure of his hopes of preferment was probably caused by his sense of its immensity and by the loss of time and strength entailed in his official employment. The greatness and variety of his task is sufficiently obvious from the foregoing chapters. He set out to endow England with poetry great in kind, in style, in thought ; conversely, to show the world that modern England was capable of poetry as great as that of any other age and country, that she had her share of poetic power, of art and learning. He brought to England the art of ancient and modern Europe : which means that he had to learn the art of Europe first—to recognize, and then to acquire and exhibit, the vital and permanent qualities that Virgil and Catullus, Petrarch and Ariosto, Marot and Ronsard, had achieved. That is one motive of imitation, and it carries with it its converse, that to prove England capable of poetry, England's poet had to meet Virgil and Ariosto and Ronsard, Rome and Italy and France, on their own ground. Certain things were held to make great poetry : England had to accomplish these things in order to take her place of credit in the eyes of the world, Spenser to accomplish them for her in order to prove himself the poet. It was a tremendous undertaking, and the more tremendous for the refusal to abandon England's own inheritance, her mode of romance and the art of Chaucer. And Spenser had to begin with the foundations, to make language and style and verse anew, to reconcile the native speech and the native taste with the style and forms of classical and foreign art, to control the violent spirit of the new age and direct it into channels of art. He saw—what every poet has known, though some modern critical schools, more concerned about psychology or metaphysics than about literature or the future of literature, fail to realize it—that the airiest vision and the clearest intuition will fail of expression if the artist have not acquired knowledge and skill in his own craft.

He laid these foundations well and truly, for all the succeeding generations of the English poets. Art is an insecure business : the poet who is hailed by all the world as the poet of England and of the sixteenth century was a younger man who worked in a strictly local and temporary form, the drama as it was evolved in the peculiar structure of the London playhouse. But Shakespeare himself might not have achieved so much if Spenser had not lived and laboured ; and after two

attempts in *Venus and Adonis* and *Lucrece*, Shakespeare
himself found he could not compete with Spenser on
Spenser's own lines.

Shakespeare's two poems fail because there is neither
feeling nor thought nor purpose to balance the heavy
decoration ; he had learned something in the school of
humanism, but not the whole lesson.   To seek and bring
home the purest honey of beauty and delight from all the
fields and gardens of art was a great work for England,
but it was not enough for the deep and ambitious mind.
Poetry for Spenser was to be an efficient cause of action
in the world, and so *The Faerie Queene* was a political
tract as well as a fine story.   That was for Spenser's
own contemporaries : but, beyond that, for all time
there should remain the moral doctrine of the poem,
working on the minds of men and inspiring them to
right thinking and right doing.   England then and for
ever should have the purest doctrine of life gathered and
stored for her use and benefit.   Spenser took for his
subject all that concerns man in all his faculties and
desires and relations, and expended all his native power
and all his acquired knowledge and skill on the construction of the ideal and on its embellishment.   Feeling, intuition, tradition, learning, the sense of beauty
and the sense of right and the sense of divinity, all combined in that ideal ; the philosophy of the ancients, the
teaching of the Church, the custom of English nobility,
were fused together.   It may be that the scholarly training was a distraction, that the true activity of the poet is
the expression of naked personal feeling, that morality
and science and philosophy should not be permitted to
intrude into art.   Yet may the fault not lie with the
conception of morality and science and philosophy that

makes them incapable of treatment in poetry? May
not thought also be experience, and must it always be set
in opposition to feeling? These things are in the
universe; must they be kept out of the poetry of one
who loves them?

For poetry, first and last, was Spenser's end and aim.
All these things might be in it, but it included and
transcended them all. That he might be a great poet,
that England might be seen among the nations in poetry
as in war and traffic and exploration, that he might
construct the comprehensive ideal of life and make it
attractive to men, Spenser studied how poetry should
be written, and first of all how it had been written. It
was no subaltern employment. Imitation means much
more than collection, for every notion of the critics, every
trick of craft, every idea of the philosophers and every
vision of delight had to approve itself to one who was
himself no mean artist, a craftsman by birth and training,
a learned thinker and a cultivated lover of beauty. So
huge a task was, of course, beyond the strength of one
man. There is confusion of thought in his work, and
still more, his various motives are apt to interfere with
one another. The delight of the senses, the keenness
of the partisan, the pleasure of thinking, the pride in
England's past and present, the love of the world and
the love of heaven are a difficult team to drive in harness,
and Spenser would not, like the reactionary Donne,
subordinate one to another even for the moment—yet
to that his instinct led him, and for him it was a failure.
There is a touch in *Mother Hubberds Tale* that we miss in
The Faerie Queene, from which it was excluded by critical
theory; there are elements in that poem which we should
like to see developed, and others which seem scarcely

worth the time spent on them. All Spenser's work, however, was in more or less degree experimental. He was always the New Poet, attempting new things. He reached his goal by the ordinary path, writing *The Court of Cupid* like any minor Chaucerian or disciple of Marot, scriptural paraphrases and *Seven Psalms* like Marot and Wyatt and Sidney and a dozen other children of the Reformation ; it is the measure of his originality that he suppressed these and followed the greater leading. He could count his failures as well as his successes, but the number, the magnitude, and the importance of his successes is token of extraordinary power ; and that power was poetic power.

To the immense task he brought immense energy. The picture which has been drawn of the gentle, impressionable Spenser warbling forth his languid strains is scarcely compatible with that of the administrator ' not unskilful or without experience in the wars '[1]—still less with the critic who traversed the most authoritative opinion in England and the poet who must have worked as few men could. This energy was the greater that it was the energy of the whole man, the patriot, the moralist, the scholar ; and since patriotism, moral feeling, scholarship were understood to be proper motives in poetry, all the force of the man wrought with the primary force of the artist to produce poetry, and all his energy was transformed into poetry. Behind this energy, inspiring and sustaining it, lay the moral qualities without which no artist may succeed—the gift of sheer hard work, patience and endurance, ambition, the determination to excel and, above all, faith and pride. The

---

[1] Letter to Irish Council recommending Spenser's appointment as Sheriff of Cork, 1598.

consummation was not only desirable, but possible. The modern age was not devoid of the qualities that make for poetry : it was as great potentially as the greatest ages of Greece and Rome ; England was as capable of breeding and nourishing poets as Greece and Rome and France and Italy ; the English language was as capable of subtlety and splendour as any that boasted their magnificence. Gabriel Harvey had his misgivings : ' What thoughe Italy, Spayne, and Fraunce, ravisshed with a certayne glorious and ambitious desier (your gallantshipp would peradventure terms it zeale and devotion) to sett oute and advaunce ther owne languages above the very Greake and Lattin, if it were possible, and standinge altogither uppon termes of honour and exquisite formes of speaches, karriinge a certayne brave magnificent grace and majestye with them, do so highly and honorablely esteeme of ther countrye poets, reposing on greate parte of their sovraigne glory and reputation abroade in the worlde in the famous writings of their nobblist wittes ? '[1]   It would not do in England, ' esspecially in Inglishe where Inglishe is contemnid, or in meeter where meeter goith a begginge.'[2] Harvey may have been right in his judgment of English carelessness and prejudice, but Mulcaster had not laboured in vain, and Spenser had faith in England and in the English tongue.

This faith in the native land and the mother tongue was but an aspect of a larger faith in poetry. Harvey judged for the present life—he seems to have been disappointed in some ambition of high appointment in the state such as the humanists of an earlier generation

[1] Draft Letter to Spenser : *Elizabethan Critical Essays*, I, 123.
[2] *Ibid.*, 135.

attained—and Spenser's material reward was unsatis-
factory. But the poet's ambition was not only for
office and wealth. He wrought for the future, in the
faith that devotion would be rewarded with immortal
fame. The belief in the immortality of poetry is the
sign and symbol of the Renaissance. The mediaeval
man, living in expectation of the inevitable end and
holding as a prime tenet of his religion that this earth
is but a fleeting bubble, dared not, could not claim for
his own work more than the brief span allotted to earthly
things :

> Al shal passe that men prose or ryme ;
> Take every man his turn, as for his time.[1]

Now the shadow had lifted, and the age of fear given
place to the age of hope and faith. Spenser had his
share of the new spirit, and the Plêiade taught him to be
bold, to believe in his mother tongue, and above all to
trust in poetry. The literary origins of this faith are
obvious enough : the phrasing of its recurrent expression can usually be traced to Ovid and Horace ; it was
a commonplace of the imitative latinists. To the new
poets it was more than an imitator's commonplace : it
was a real faith, nor was it an unreasonable faith. The
very fact of the Revival proved that Ovid and Horace
were no empty boasters. The Empire was broken up,
the City destroyed : the art of Virgil, of Horace, of
Ovid, Claudian, Lucan, Seneca, remained in all its
strength and brightness. The poets lamented of the
ruins of greatness, but *The Ruines of Rome* is followed by
The Ruines of Time, and poetry is proclaimed the one
permanent monument of human greatness.

[1] Chaucer, *Envoy to Scogan.*

For deeds doe die, however noblie donne,
And thoughts of men doe as them selves decay ;
But wise wordes taught in numbers for to runne,
Recorded by the Muses, live for aye,
Ne may with storming showres be washt away,
Ne bitter breathing windes with harmful blast,
Nor age, nor envy, shall them ever wast.[1]

Holding such a faith the poet might well be proud,
over whom, alone among men, Mutability held no sway,
who could even save others from devouring Oblivion.
Of all compliments paid to Elizabeth it was the highest
that Spenser should ' dedicate, present and consecrate '
his Heroic Poem ' to live with the eternitie of her
fame.'

The precedent of the elder poets was authority enough
for the claim to immortality, the historical fact evidence
enough that it was well based. The pride and the
common sense of the new poets discovered that the
secret of immortality was not in the prestige of language
or time, but in poetry, the universal spirit which may
move in any land and inspire any tongue and vouchsafe
to any age a measure of its authentic power. And
beyond literary precedent and historical evidence the
new poets had the greatest of reasons for their faith and
their pride : in their eyes poetry was the gift of God,
bestowed in His mysterious grace upon a few favoured
mortals, ' a divine gift and heavenly instinct not to bee
gotten by laboure and learning, but adorned with both ;
and poured into the witte by a certain Ἐνθουσιασμὸς and
celestiall inspiration.'[2]

---

[1] *Ruines of Time*, 400–406.
[2] E. K., Argument to *October*.

Par art le navigateur
Dans la mer manie, et vire
La bride de son navire :
Par art plaide l'Orateur,
Par art les Rois sont guerriers,
Par art se font les ouvriers ;
Mais si vaine experience
Vous n'aurez de tel erreur,
Sans plus ma sainte fureur
Polira vostre science . . .

       les vers viennent de Dieu,
    Non de l'humaine puissance.[1]

Thus in Ronsard's fable Jupiter addresses the Muses, breathing into them the gift of poetry which they are to communicate to the elect among men.

Une fureur d'esprit au ciel me conduisoit
D'une aile qui la mort et les siecles evite,
Et le docte troppeau qui sur Parnasse habite
De son feu plus divin mon ardeur attisoit.[2]

Such secret comfort, and such heavenly pleasures,
Ye sacred imps that on Parnaso dwell,
And there the keeping have of learnings threasures,
Which doe the worldly riches farre excell,
Into the mindes of mortall men do well
And goodly fury into them infuse.[3]

The idea was old, older than Ovid, who supplied the Emblem to *October, Agitante calescimus illo, etc.* 'This science can not grow but by some divine instinct—the Platonicks call it *furor.*'[4] Sidney cites the original

---

[1] Ronsard, *Ode à Michel de l'Hospital*, Epodes, 12, 14.
[2] Du Bellay, *Les Regrets*, vii.
[3] *Faerie Queene*, Book VI, Introduction, ii.
[4] Puttenham, in *Elizabethan Critical Essays*, II, p. 3.

authority : ' Plato . . . in his Dialogue called *Ion*, giveth high and rightly divine commendation to Poetrie . . . especially sith he attributeth unto Poesie more than my selfe doe, namely, to be a very inspiring of a divine force, farre above mans wit, as in the afore-named Dialogue is apparent.'[1] Puttenham was uncertain; Sidney, though sympathetic, sceptical ; the new poets believed. To the Pléiade and to Spenser the Muses represent something more real and more powerful than the decorative image they soon became in the neo-classic poetry of both countries, for, as we have seen, they represent the power of God.

Poetry, then, was a high calling, reserved for the elect. Ronsard ' commonly said that all men should not rashly concern themselves with poetry ; that prose was the language of men, but poetry was the language of the gods ; and that men should not be its interpreters unless they were consecrated from their birth and dedicated to this ministry.'[2] It is this sense of vocation that divides the Renaissance poets from the mediaeval, and which, still more, sets Spenser apart from the group of courtier poets who were his early patrons, as it made him the acknowledged leader of the Elizabethan poets and, in the words of his epitaph, ' the Prince of Poets in his Tyme.' Thence came the intense conviction of the value of his work and the confidence in its reward. The poet was the chosen agent of God, and in return for faithful service he was granted a measure of the permanence which is in God alone. That was the ultimate inspiration of his labour and the source of energy ; and that was the responsibility which rested upon him. The poet was responsible for his country as a nursery of

---

[1] Sidney, *ibid.*, I, p. 192.   [2] Binet, *Vie de Ronsard*.

poetry ; for his native tongue ; for the truth and sound-
ness of his doctrine ; for the action it prompted and the
desires it aroused and the thought it directed. He was
responsible to the Giver that his talent was sedulously
cultivated and worthily employed. So while Spenser
gave to England, to his contemporaries and his followers,
the example of a magnificent way of writing, of art and
thought, of a strenuous working life, he gave what was
even more valuable—pride and confidence, the fervour
of conviction and faith.

Appendix

SPENSER'S METRES

A. The Metres of *The Shepheardes Calender*.

(1) 10-line stanza $a_{12}b_{10}a_{10}b_{10}b_{10}c_8c_8x_4b_{10}x_4$ *Nov.* song.
    var. a b a b a c c x a x in the 5th stanza.

(2) 9-line stanza $a_{10}b_4a_{10}b_4c_{10}c_{10}d_5d_5c_8$ *Apr.* song.

(3) 8-line stanza $a_{10}b_{10}a_{10}b_{10}b_{10}a_{10}b_{10}a_{10}$ *June.*

(4) 6-line stanza $a_{10}b_{10}b_{10}a_{10}b_{10}a_{10}$ *Oct.*

(5) 6-line stanza $a_{10}b_{10}a_{10}b_{10}c_{10}c_{10}$ *Jan., Aug.* dialogue, *Dec.*

(6) 6-line stanza $a_8a_8b_6a_8a_8b_6$ *March.*

(7) 4-line stanza $a_{10}b_{10}a_{10}b_{10}$ *Apr.* dial., *Nov.* dial. (linked).

(8) 4-line stanza $a_8b_6a_8b_6$ *July.*

(9) 4-line stanza $a_8b_5a_8b_7$ *Aug.* song.

(10) couplet   8-syllable   *To His Booke.*

(11) couplet   12-syllable   *Envoy.*

(12) couplet   "Chaucerian" or four-beat   *Feb., May, Sept.*

(13) sestina   10-syllable   *Aug.*

(14) uncertain   12-syllable   Gloss on *Oct.*, line 90.

B. Rhyme-Schemes.

(1) Non-lyrical:

Faerie Queene	9-line	a b a b b c b c c
June	8-line	a b a b b a b a

189

V. Gnat ; Muio.　8-line　a b a b a b c c
R. Time ;
　Hymnes　　　7-line　a b a b b c c
　Daphnaida　　,,　　a b a b c b c
Jan. ; Aug. dial. ;
Dec., ; T.M. ;
　Astr.　　　　6-line　a b a b c c
　Oct.　　　　　,,　　a b b a b a

(2) Lyrical (short lines *in italics*) :

Nov. song　　10-line　a b a b b c *c x* b *x*
April song　　9-line　*a b a b* c c *d d* c
Epithalamion 17–19 line
　all stanzas begin　a b a b c *c* d c d . . .
　12 19-line stanzas
　　　　　　continue　　. . . *e e* f g g f h *h* x x
　1　,,　　stanza
　　　　　continues　　. . . *e e* f g f g h *h* x x
　5 18-line stanzas
　　　　　　continue　　. . . *e e* f g g f *f* x x
　3　,,　　stanzas
　　　　　　continue　　. . . *d* e f f e g *g* x x
　1 17-line stanza
　　　　　continues　　. . . e f f e g g x x
Prothalamion　18-line
　all stanzas begin　a b b a *a* . . .
　6 stanzas continue　. . . c d c d *d e* e f e *f f* x x
　3　,,　　　,,　　. . . b c b c *c* d d e d *e e* x x
　1 stanza continues　. . . c b c b *b* d d e d *e e* x x

(3) Sonnets :

Rome ; Bellay ; Petrarch　a b a b c d c d e f e f g g　7 rhymes
Rome, L'Envoy　　a b a b c d c d d e d e f f　6 rhymes
Bellay, sonnet 11　　a b a b c b c b d e d e f f　,,　　,,
　　,,　　,,　7　　a b a b b c b c d e d e f f　,,　　,,

Sonnet before *Castriot*	a b a b c d c d e d e d f f	6 rhymes
Petrarch, sonnet 7 ; *Amoretti* ;		
before *F.Q.* ; to Har-		
vey ; before *Venice*	a b a b b c b c c d c d e e	5 rhymes
before *Nennio*	a b a b b b b b b c b c d d	4 rhymes

C. Lyrical Stanzas.

Madrigal 1
6-line $a_8 b_6 a_8 b_9 c_8 c_9$

Madrigal 2
8-line $a_8 a_8 b_6 a_8 a_8 b_6 c_8 c_8$

Madrigal 3
8-line $a_8 a_8 b_9 a_8 a_8 b_9 c_8 c_9$

April song
9-line $a_{10} b_4 a_{10} b_4 c_{10} c_{10} d_5 d_5 c_8$

Madrigal 4
10-line $a_{11} b_6 a_{11} b_6 c_{10} d_6 c_{10} d_6 e_8 e_8$

Nov. song
10-line $a_{12} b_{10} a_{10} b_{10} b_{10} c_8 c_8 x_4 b_{10} x_4$

Prothalamion
18-line $a_{10} b_{10} b_{10} a_{10} a_6 c_{10} d_{10} c_{10} d_{10} d_6 e_{10} e_{10} f_{10} e_{10} f_6 f_6 x_{10} x_{10}$
     or $a_{10} b_{10} b_{10} a_{10} a_6 b_{10} c_{10} b_{10} c_{10} c_6 d_{10} d_{10} e_{10} d_{10} e_6 e_6 x_{10} x_{10}$

Epithalamion
18-line $a_{10} b_{10} a_{10} b_{10} c_{10} c_6 d_{10} c_{10} d_{10} e_{10} e_6 f_{10} g_{10} g_{10} f_{10} f_6 x_{10} x_{12}$
     or $a_{10} b_{10} a_{10} b_{10} c_{10} c_6 d_{10} c_{10} d_{10} d_6 e_{10} f_{10} f_{10} e_{10} g_{10} g_6 x_{10} x_{12}$
19-line $a_{10} b_{10} a_{10} b_{10} c_{10} c_6 d_{10} c_{10} d_{10} e_{10} e_6 f_{10} g_{10} g_{10} f_{10} h_{10} h_6 x_{10} x_{12}$

NOTES

In *A* and *C* above the French syllabic verse-notation is used. This is merely for convenience in printing, and without prejudice to any system the reader may prefer. Spenser's variations in respect of number are not accounted for in the Table ; they are easily observed.

A tabulates the remarks in the text, page 98.

B illustrates Spenser's experiments in rhyme-schemes, and their development from the basis *a b a b.* The variations in the *November* Song, *Epithalamion,*[1] *Prothalamion,* and the Sonnets (especially the obvious blunder of the sonnet contributed to *Nennio*) show, like the rhyme-schemes of *June* and *October* and the opening of *Colin Clout (a b a b c b c . . .)* and the occasional linking of quatrains in the same poem, a constant tendency in Spenser to repeat the same rhymes. This is one effect of his dependence upon the ear ; it seems as if he were trying to use the minimum number of rhymes, or to show that English was not so deficient in rhymes as some alleged. The structure *a b b a a . . .* with which *Prothalamion* opens is used by Petrarch in three (out of 29) *canzoni,* but his general tendency is to introduce a greater variety of rhymes early in his scheme, and to keep his rhyme-words far apart. According to the rule of the *canzone,* of course, the structure of every stanza should be the same, but we may take it Spenser was not trying to write strict Italian *canzoni* in English, any more than strict Petrarchan sonnets.

[1] The break in the rhyme-scheme at line 192 is more apparent than real : though all editions have *womanhood,* we should clearly read *womanhead,* of which Osgood's *Concordance* gives nine examples in Spenser, as against five (other) examples of *womanhood.*

C illustrates Spenser's experiments in what King James called 'broken and cuttit verses.' The *Madrigals* are the little poems or *odelettes* found between *Amoretti* and *Epithalamion* ; they are called *Epigrams* in the Globe edition, but the ordinary Petrarchan term is surely preferable.

It is worthy of observation that, so far as we know, Spenser never attempted to revive the old lyrical forms rondel and ballade, which died with Wyatt and the school of Marot. He might have continued this part of the Chaucer tradition if he had cared ; but the artificial forms connoted the trivialities of the decadence, they were superseded by Italian modes and despised by the Pléiade, and a new lyrical tradition was growing with the growth of music.

INDEX